THE IMPACT OF WORLD WAR ONE
ON THE JEWISH PEOPLE

The Impact of

WORLD WAR ONE

on the Jewish People

Larry Domnitch

URIM PUBLICATIONS
Jerusalem • New York

The Impact of World War One on the Jewish People

by Larry Domnitch

Copyright © 2020 Larry Domnitch

Typeset by Ariel Walden

Printed in Israel

First Edition

ISBN 978-1-60280-374-9

Urim Publications
P.O. Box 52287
Jerusalem 9152102
Israel

www.UrimPublications.com

Library of Congress Cataloging-in-Publication Data

Names: Domnitch, Larry, author.
Title: The impact of World War One on the Jewish people / Larry Domnitch.
Description: First edition. | Jerusalem ; New York : Urim Publications, [2019]
| Includes bibliographical references. | Summary: "The First World War and
its aftermath had a calamitous impact on the Jewish people, whether on the
battlefields or as refugees. Age-old hatreds were reignited. This is the history of a
traumatic period often not given sufficient attention, having been eclipsed by the
enormity of the Holocaust."— Provided by publisher.
Identifiers: LCCN 2019041396 | ISBN 9781602803749 (hardcover)
Subjects: LCSH: World War, 1914-1918—Jews—Europe. | World War, 1914-
1918—Participation, Jewish. | Jews—Europe—History—20th century. | World
War, 1914-1918—Social aspects—Europe. | Europe—Ethnic relations—Histo-
ry—20th century.
Classification: LCC D639.J4 D66 2019 | DDC 940.3089/92404—dc23
LC record available at https://lccn.loc.gov/2019041396

Dedicated to my parents,

HAROLD and LORRAINE DOMNITCH

I would like to thank my wife Tova,
who assisted with the editing.
Her input and suggestions
greatly enhanced the manuscript.

Contents

A Note to the Reader   9
Introduction   11

Chapter 1 War Breaks Out   13
         2 The Germans Advance East into Poland   36
         3 How Long is the Night?   66
         4 Under German Occupation   99
         5 Encounters   110
         6 Fundraising   120
         7 Letters from German Soldiers at the Front   126
         8 Excerpts and Letters from the Anglo Jewish
            Press About the Troops   134
         9 Austria   141
        10 The Russian Revolution   147
        11 The Yanks Are Coming   151
        12 Zion   154
        13 A Jewish Army: The First in Almost
            Two Thousand Years   163
        14 Aftermath of the Armistice   198

"The Lord gazes upon the Earth and it trembles."
Psalms 104:32

Europe Before the First World War, 1871–1914. (*Wikimedia*)

A Note to the Reader

The First World War was a time of transformation for the world when empires and nations engaged in warfare on a massive scale that was unprecedented in history.

It was also a time of trauma for the Jewish people who were caught in the middle of the conflagration.

It is my intention to present descriptions and accounts in this volume to provide the reader with a closer view of how the events of the First World War impacted world Jewry. Very often, the events surrounding the First World War are not given sufficient attention, eclipsed by the enormity of the Holocaust. Millions of Jews were personally affected by World War I, whether upon the battlefields, by being in close proximity to the fighting, or as refugees. The era of the First World War ignited existing age-old hatreds against Jews throughout the world, and posed unprecedented challenges in a world rife with peril. The Jews during the war, often as in history, were in close proximity to the middle of the chaos, witnessing and bearing much of its horrors, while hoping and endeavoring for a better future.

Rabbi Yehudah Leib Graubart, in the introduction of a book he authored on the extreme difficulties of the First World War, cited a sentence from the Psalms, "Hashem looks to the Earth and it trembles." (104:32) The Hebrew word for "The Earth *trembles*" – *tirad* – has a numerical equivalent of the year, 5674, which is 1914.[1]

As so many other descendants of so many European Jews who

---

1. Yehudah Leib Graubart, *Sefer Zikaron* (Book of Remembrance), Druk. Ch. Wein, Lodz, 1926, Introduction.

immigrated to the West, my parents' families were profoundly affected by the war.

My paternal grandfather, Julius Domnitch, as so many immigrants at the time, arrived at American shores with the expectation that he would soon be able to bring his wife Goldie and their young son, Irving. Those plans were put on hold due to financial strains, and then the war broke out. My grandmother, perhaps fearing an impending pogrom in their home town of Luninetz in Belorussia, fled and found refuge in a German internment camp.

My maternal grandmother, Sheindal (Jenny) Merkur, from the town of Brezany in Galitzia, also experienced the nightmare of being in the proximity of the war. With the approach of invading Russian forces, the peaceful life her family had known had come to an abrupt end. Near their home, pitch battles were waged. Like so many others, they were forced to flee from their home as refugees. While in transit, one of her brothers was apprehended and executed – possibly on the false suspicion so often leveled against Jews of being a spy. Her father was falsely imprisoned by Russian forces, where he would die soon after.

Some of her surviving family members served in the military of Austria-Hungary.

Their travails were similar to the plight of so many other Jewish families at the time.

May their memories be for a blessing.

Introduction

September 30, 1914. Yom Kippur was approaching and Jewish soldiers in a battalion asked their commander for permission to gather and pray together. Their request was granted and they gathered in an empty storehouse for services.

They prayed with heightened emotion and shed bitter tears over their difficult plight as soldiers on the front. Also prominent on their minds was the welfare of their families in Poland and Russia facing untold dangers due to the war.

When the time for the concluding prayer, *Ne'ila*, arrived, a young soldier named Aronchik was asked to serve as *chazzan*.[2]

It was a very special *Ne'ila* service. Aronchik's prayers were powerful; his voice melodic and piercing. The emotions emitted by his prayers were indescribable. Everyone present shed a river of tears as they pleaded for their lives in the face of the horrors of combat. Soon the fast was over, but no one rushed to eat. Everyone just sat contemplating the intensity of their prayers. Black bread and tea were finally brought and the soldiers broke their fast, yet the *chazzan* who had aroused them to repentance did not partake.

With the fast and the day over, the soldiers laid down on the ground, exhausted, but they could not sleep as they were anxious about the battles that lay ahead.

The following day a new battle erupted. The fighting was furious. The cannons began pounding and the bullets flew like hail. Men were falling all around; one never knew which moment might be his last.

---

2. The last of the five major prayers recited on Yom Kippur; it is traditionally recited just before sundown.

Eventually the fighting stopped and the enemy retreated. The soldiers began to regroup and were horrified to see that Aronchik, the *Ba'al Ne'ila*, had fallen.

A grave was dug for him by his Jewish comrades, giving him his final honor. On his gravestone they wrote, "Here lies Aronchik, the '*Baal Ne'ila*'; May his righteous soul rest in peace."[3]

---

3. Shimon Zev Eizenberg, *Milchomo Shtoib*, (War Dust), *Zichronos Fun a Yiddishe Palit* 1915–1917, (Memoirs of a Jewish Refugee), Klerksdorf Publishers, South Africa, 1922, pp. 30–33.

Chapter 1

War Breaks Out

Background

The First World War was a global conflagration that had shaken the world so violently that it continues to tremble even today. It was a massive storm whose affects are still felt. The carnage of the war was unprecedented in the annals of human history, testing the limits of the destruction human beings could inflict upon others.

Unsanitary disease ridden trenches became the abode to millions of troops. There, they endured incessant massive artillery bombardments with new ranges and explosiveness, inflicting enormous destruction as they awaited the dreaded call to attack in reckless, over the top, charges into enemy fire. Improved machine guns could cut down waves of infantry attacks. The Germans introduced poison gas as a weapon adding to the horrors on the battlefield. The British began using tanks at the battle of the Somme in 1916. Airplanes were used to control the skies causing terror and destruction. Communications by telephone helped armed forces better coordinate. In a prolonged war, forces armed with modern weaponry faced each other at close proximity producing even greater catastrophic consequences.

World War I followed the industrial revolution which transformed weaponry into modern efficient killing machines. It also followed two centuries of enlightenment, which emphasized the rights and equality of man. They were times for contemplation of a more humane world. World War one came as a storm which plunged mankind into horrific new era of darkness; testifying to mankind's enduring capacity for destruction.

The First World War also caused massive civilian casualties due to the proximity of the fighting to civilian populations. Civilians were often victims of bombardments and harassment by troops. Warfare was accompanied by persecution and displacement, often by decree, which caused a flood of refugees throughout Europe. Scorched-earth policies enforced more often by the Russians upon their retreats, destroyed anything of potential use to the enemy and left masses of homeless refugees in flight. Because supplies were limited, starvation and disease often ensued. Over the course of the war, over nine million troops died, 23 million persons were wounded, and there were about six to eight million civilian deaths, due mostly to starvation and disease.

Allied nations of the Entente alliance went to war offering justifications in the name of humanity; to protect smaller nations like Belgium and Bosnia from German aggression and to free the world from the threat of the Kaiser. The often stated goal of Germany was to free Eastern Europe from the tyranny of Russian oppression under the Czars. The "cultured" Germans thought they were going to civilize humanity, but in actuality, Germany felt threatened by its neighbors. The Kaiser had implied that Germany was forced into war for self-preservation when he stated, "I raise the sword that has been thrust in my hand."[1] All sides believed that a defensive war was imposed upon them. However, more than anything else, Germany in the aftermath of its 1871 unification of smaller Prussian provinces, sought to realize its vision of building a massive empire.

The Causes

There were a combination of factors which led to the start of World War One. Nations involved perceived themselves as being pulled into the fray by global considerations.

In 1870, the Franco-Prussian War between France and Germany left France without its material-rich buffer zone, the Alsace Lorraine

---

1. Amos Elon, *The Pity of it All; A Portrait of the German Jewish Ethic: 1743–1933*, Picador/Henry Holt and Co., New York, 2002, p. 301

province on the border between the two nations. The resentment was deep. France wanted to regain possession of the territory.

Several European nations competed over colonies in Africa, Asia, and the Americas, within which lands were acquired. Colonialism, as it is known, increased in the 1880s. The leading colonial power was Great Britain where "the sun never set," over its massive empire. By 1900, 90% of Africa was controlled by European nations. The competition between Great Britain and Germany, as well as Germany and France over colonies in Africa led to disputes and increased naval forces in order to protect trade routes. There was also the fear that a competing power would acquire too much wealth and pose a military threat.

Another factor was the increase of nationalist sentiment. During the 19th century, people who spoke the same language and had the same culture often sought a common national identity through independence. Much of nationalism was based upon contemporary political ideas which emphasized nationality as a means of keeping societies united. This wave swept through Europe uniting smaller provinces into nations. First in France during the French Revolution, then other peoples followed such as Greece, Belgium, Poland, Italy, Hungary, Germany, Bulgaria, Romania, Serbia, Ireland and Montenegro. Considering themselves an integral part of their nation, citizens were prepared to fight spurred by feelings of patriotism. With stronger national identifications, conflicts more readily arose by nationalistic ethnic groups in order to achieve or to preserve their independence.

Distrust and economic competition led to alliances, which often widened conflicts. The first modern European alliance was formed in 1879 between Germany and Austria-Hungary. The Austro-Hungarian Empire, a duel monarchy comprised of nations sharing power which had been formed in 1867 had feared a Russian attack, while the Germans feared that France would try to take back Alsace Lorraine. In 1894, France and Russia allied themselves against Germany. Italy (which changed sides in 1915) then joined the alliance with Germany in order to protect her colonial interests in Tunisia, North Africa, from the French. In 1907, the Triple Entente was formed with Great Britain joining the Russian/ French alliance over concern with the increased militarization of Germany. Great Britain's entry into the alliance was based upon the loosely worded term, "moral obligation" in the event of war, however, the British were well aware that without alliances, their empire was in danger. Germany, as a result, felt surrounded and vulnerable.

A dangerous arms race spread throughout the European continent. The military build-up by nations at enormous expense and modern technological weaponry made the prospect of war all the more dangerous and possible due to increasing mistrust between alliances. Germany feared the armaments of Russia, while Great Britain feared the growing naval power of Germany.

By 1913, the German Kaiser Wilhelm II was primed for war amassing an army of over 600,000. Other nations had also prepared. Most did not see the catastrophe that lay ahead. These were peaceful times for Europe, which hadn't seen a war in decades.

The Spark Which Ignited the Conflagration

The nephew of the Austro/Hungarian Emperor, Archduke Franz Ferdinand, was a reformist who had considered accommodation with the Serbians, a national entity within the empire which sought independence. But events in the Serbian capital, Sarajevo, would ensure that his plans would not be realized.

On a visit to Sarajevo, Serbia, on June 28, 1914, the Archduke had survived an attempted assassination by members of the Black Hand, a radical separatist group seeking Serbian independence. After a reception in his honor, Ferdinand set out to the city hospital to visit those wounded in the attack. However, while the Archduke's motorcade took an alternate route to the hospital to avoid the dangers of another assassination attempt, his driver was unaware of the changed route. As the car turned onto Franz Joseph Street (ironically named after the Emperor) an accompanying passenger, General Oskar Potiorek, had noticed that the planned route was not taken and notified the driver, who began to reverse the car. Gavrilo Princip, a member of the Black Hand, happened to be in a café on the street at the moment. At point blank range, he aimed his gun at the royal couple. The bullets he fired struck the Archduke in the neck, and his wife

Sophie, who was sitting by his side, in the abdomen. The couple died soon after.

Riots followed the assassination in Sarajevo and other places within Austria/Hungary against the Serbs, and Serbia was blamed. It is conceivable that the Serbian government had backed the assassins. A tenuous relationship between the two was now challenged. At the time, the German Kaiser was on vacation.

A few weeks later, the Austro-Hungarians, not in a conciliatory mood, hardened their positions and demanded that the Serbian government accept an Austro-Hungarian investigation into the assassination, and that Austria should be involved in the entire judicial process in trying the assassins. These demands were rejected by Serbia, considering it an affront to their aspirations for independence. Serbia replied that it is not a province of the Austro-Hungarian Empire. On July 28, 1914, one month to the day after the archduke and wife were killed, Austria-Hungary declared war on Serbia initiating a regional war. However, Russia was the protector of Serbia and all Slavic nations and on account of the alliances, the conflict would soon spread.

Austria-Hungary attacked on this day with an artillery barrage. The Serbians turned to their ally, Russia, which sent troops to the Austrian border. Kaiser Wilhelm of Germany gave the Austro-Hungarians assurances that Germany would come to her aid if needed, although he did not think that Russia or France were sufficiently prepared to actually join in a fight. On August 1, Germany and Russia declared war on each other. Also ready to back Russia was France, bound by treaty.

The following day on August 2, the German army invaded Luxemburg and demanded the right to invade neutral Belgium. On August 3, Germany declared war on France and invaded Belgium, which bordered on France. On August 4, the Germans officially declared war on Belgium, hoping for a quick victory on the Western front. Great Britain, in turn, honoring an 1839 agreement to defend Belgium if attacked, declared war on Germany.

European nations and their colonies were plunged into war. Initially, the expectation was that the war would not last as each side believed it would quickly achieve victory. The German Kaiser, Wilhelm II confidently told his troops they will be home "before the leaves fall."[2] Such optimism was of course premature. He grossly underestimated his opponents, not believing that Russia was prepared to fight, that Great Britain was actually willing to join the war, or that Belgium would mount a significant resistance after being invaded. A global catastrophe was in the making.

Following the outbreak of war in 1914, German forces ravaged towns upon the invasion of Belgium whose forces bravely resisted. In the city of Louvain, Belgium, from August 25 to 30, the entire town was demolished and its' population of ten thousand were expelled. Other Belgium towns met similar fates. To the south of Europe, as the war broke out, 4,000 Serbian civilians were massacred by invading Austrian troops. More horrors followed. Entire populations of Armenians were massacred and forced to face starvation by the Ottoman Turks. The number of Armenian deaths were about one and a half million.

Some saw the looming disaster. Lord Edward Grey of Fallodon, who served as the British Foreign Secretary from 1905 to 1916, observed on August 3, 1914, "The lamps are going out all over Europe; we shall not see them lit again in our time."[3]

The Jews

The Jewish people were in close proximity to the conflict.

The First World War, which began on August 1, 1914 when the major powers, Germany and Russia declared war on each other, was also the ill-fated day of mourning – Tisha B'Av – the ninth day of the month of Av which commemorates the long history of Jewish suffering. On Tisha B'Av, the First and Second Jerusalem Temples were destroyed, and the last stronghold of the Bar Kochba revolt, the Judean city of Betar, fell to the Romans in 135 CE.

In 1914, Tisha B'Av fell on the Sabbath, and observance of the fast was pushed off to Sunday, in accordance with Jewish law. Just days before the official declarations of war, the London Jewish Chronicle

---

2. Ibid. Amos Elan, p. 298

3. Hew Strachen, *The Origins of the First World War*, Oxford University Press, 2004, p.223

poignantly noted the approaching day of Tisha B'Av with a fore-boding tone, "Politically, the Jew is today still suffering in his own condition the consequences of the overthrow of 2,000 years ago. The homelessness which then began still continues, with all the manifold disabilities and tragedies that spring inevitably from it. Religiously, again, the loss of home has meant and still means, exposure to an increasingly hostile environment, with results that are writ large in the records of our time."[4]

In 1914, world Jewry numbered about fourteen million. Over six million Jews resided within the Russian empire. Most were confined to the regions of Russian Republics and Czarist-controlled Poland, otherwise known as the "Pale Settlement," the land mass where the Jews had been confined by the Czars for the previous one hundred and twenty years since the reign of the Czarina Catherine the Great. Almost three million Jews resided in the United States, and two and a half million resided within the Austria-Hungarian Empire. Six hundred thousand lived in Germany, and three hundred thousand in Romania. In Great Britain, Jews numbered 245,000, France, 100,000, and in Palestine they numbered between 90,000 and 95,000. About 400,000 Jews resided in North Africa. In Asia, outside of Palestine, there were an additional 250,000. There were also sizable Jewish communities in South and Central America, Italy, Canada, Australia, New Zealand and South Africa.[5]

World War I had a devastating impact upon the Jewish People. The Jews were often specifically targeted for persecution because of their identity as Jews. Throughout history, Jewish communities faced many destructive and spurious accusations which led to persecution. These included blood libels, in which Jews were accused of murdering local children; desecrations of the Host, where Jews were accused of damaging the wafers used in church services; and being part of cabals seeking world domination, as espoused in the infamous Protocols of the Elders of Zion. During the First World War, Jews faced incessant charges of treason. Such accusations were

---

4. London Jewish Chronicle, July 31, 1914, p. 7

5. Abraham Ducker, Contemporary Jewish Record, Vol. 2, 1939, "Jews in the World War: A Brief Historical Sketch" p. 8

often leveled by the Russian army, its leadership and by ordinary Russian and Polish citizens. As a result, Jews found themselves facing devastating pogroms, and wholesale expulsions.

The economic downturn as a result of the upheavals disrupted the lives of hundreds of thousands of Jewish families. Likewise, hundreds of Jewish cities and towns were destroyed in the bitter fighting. The devastation also caused a demoralization of much of world Jewry. The religious life of Eastern European Jewry was dealt a crushing blow to institutions that preserve Jewish life. The Synagogue, the Yeshiva, the *cheder* (primary school), and the community, were largely uprooted and damaged as a result.

Following the start of the war, as the German army moved eastward into the Pale Settlement, the Jews would be relieved of the persecution at the hands of the Russians, but under German control they would still face harsh rule and the devastating tragedies of hunger and disease. To make matters even worse, areas to which the Russian army retreated also saw a massive wave of destructive pogroms and expulsions as many blamed the Jews for Russia's defeats.

The total number of combatants in World War I was 65 million. About 1.5 million Jews fought comprising over 2% of the total. Among the 42,000,000 fighting men for the allies, 2.5% were Jews; of the 23,000,000 troops in the Central Powers, 450,000 or 2% were Jews.[6] The number of Jews who fell in action was 170,825. Of that number 116,825 were in the allied armies, otherwise known as the Entente, and 54,000 were killed fighting for the Central Powers. Over 400,000 were wounded in action. The proportion of Jews who died on the battlefields approximated their percentage in the armies.[7]

The hope for acceptance, of achieving equality, of ending age-old anti-Semitic stereotypes was a driving force for many Jews volunteering in the army before drafts were enforced adding impetus to their patriotism at this time. During an era of heightened nationalism, many Jews sought to prove their worthiness by their service. Change in attitudes towards the Jews seemed to be forthcoming.

---

6. Abraham Ducker, Contemporary Jewish Record, Vol. 2, 1939, "Jews in the World War: A Brief Historical Sketch" p. 8

7. Ibid. p. 9

Contemporary pronouncements of some world leaders who called for acceptance of minorities, which included the Jews added credence to that perception.

In Germany, which at that time seemed united to include different classes and minorities, the German Kaiser Wilhelm II, from the balcony of the Royal Palace on August 1, 1914, proclaimed that he "no longer recognizes any German parties. . . . Today we are all Germans brothers and only German brothers."[8]

When the war broke out, the Russian Czar, Nicholas II, seeking support from the almost six million Jews who resided within the Russian Empire, issued an appeal entitled, "My Dear Jews" which offered long awaited promises of equality.[9] Many Jews responded enthusiastically by sending funds to the war effort, establishing hospitals, and encouraging young men to enlist.[10]

In Germany

An appeal to German Jewry by the Imperial Association of German Jews stated:

> German Jews, in this fateful hour it is once again time to show that proud of our lineage, We Jews are among the best sons of our fatherland. The noblest of our millennia Old history obliges. We expect our young to hasten to the colors voluntarily and with high hearts. German Jews! We appeal to you, in the spirit of the old Jewish rule of duty, to dedicate yourselves to the service of your fatherland with all your heart, all your soul, and all your abilities.[11]

At the onset of the war, German Jewish poet, writer, and playwright,

---

8. WWW.GermanHistoryDocuments, "Wilhemine Germany and the First World War"

9. Ducker, Contemporary Jewish Record, Ibid. p. 9

10. The American Jewish Committee, "The Jews of the Eastern War Zone," Jewish Publication Society America, Philadelphia, PA, 1916, p. 37

11. Rachel Salamander, *The Jewish World of Yesterday*, Rizzoli Publishers, New York, 1991, p. 260

Ernst Lissauer, echoed the sentiments of many German Jews. Angered by the British blockade of Germany, he composed an enormously popular "Hymn of Hatred" against Great Britain. One stanza states, "Never is our hatred going to abate. Hatred on the sea, hatred on the land. Hatred of the head, hatred on the hand."[12] The Kaiser himself bestowed a medal upon Lissauer. After the rise of Nazism in 1933, Lissauer immigrated to Austria where he was deprived of his German citizenship by the Nazis. Before he died in 1937, he expressed regret for having written the song, which he had hastily crafted in a Hamburg Café, while caught up in the emotions and anger at the times.[13]

Loyalty to Germany's cause was shared by most of German Jewry and German Jewish contributions were significant.

With the words "This war will introduce a new era in Germany."[14] Ludwig Frank, a prominent Jewish member of the Reichstag (German Parliament) volunteered in August and was among the first casualties. Frank spoke of his devotion and that he was glad to let his blood flow for the fatherland. Quoted in a column from a German newspaper, he offered an outlook into the future, "We trust in the final valid victory of German arms and in the glorious peace which we are helping to attain by fighting. We rejoice in the fraternization of Jews and Christians which is bound to spread at home. We are sure that after such soulful experiences that after this storm tried fellowship the flame of the old hatred will not blaze up again."[15] He continued, "German character and conduct shall once again make the world well again."[16]

German scientist Fritz Haber developed the use of poison gas in war. Richard Willstatter, a chemist, and Nobel Prize recipient for research in plant pigments, especially chlorophyll, was asked by

---

12. Howard M. Sachar, *Dreamland: Europeans and Jews in the Aftermath of the Great War*, Vintage Books, New York, 2002, pp. 218–219

13. Jewish Telegraphic Agency, December 13, 1937. Lissauer like so many German Jews at his time had accepted Christianity. He later returned to Judaism.

14. B'nai B'rith News, November, 1915, "The War and the German Jews," by Dr. S. Behrens. p. 4

15. Ibid.

16. Ibid.

Haber to develop a gas mask, which he did. For that he was awarded the iron cross.[17] Due to rising anti-Semitism, he stepped down from his position at the University of Berlin in protest in 1924. Both men managed to flee Nazi Germany in the late 1930s.[18]

German Jews were at the forefront of purchasing war bonds.[19] Ludwig Spiegel, an elderly veteran of the Franco-Prussian war of 1870, insisted on joining his own regiment.[20]

The Kaiser had proclaimed August 5 a day of prayer, and synagogues obliged as Rabbis led prayers for the fatherland.[21]

At the same time, the precipitous fall of German Jewry had begun.

By late 1914, Jewish newspapers began to complain about anti-Semitic slander published in the press. The next year, the right wing Pan German League and the Farmer's League dropped all restraint and engaged in blatant anti-Semitism, claiming that the Jews shirked responsibility and profiteered from the war.[22] As troubles in Germany increased so would the blame.

While the Western Front would be locked in a stalemate, with enormous German casualties, the mood in Germany was further deteriorating. By October 11, 1916, the tone towards Germany's Jews began to show signs of significant change. Manifestations of increasing anti-Semitism were apparent as the German War Department claimed to receive numerous complaints that Jews shirked military service, and staged a "Jew count" to count Jewish casualties. The purpose was to impugn the loyalty of German Jewry by underestimating the level of participation and losses of German Jews. It began when an anti-Semitic representative in the German Parliament addressed a question to the Minister of War, Adolf Wild von Hohenborn, of "How many Jews are serving at the front?" The intent was to negatively portray the Jews as shirkers who served in the back lines and

17. W. Michael Blumenthal, *The Invisible Wall, Germans and Jews: A Personal Exploration*, Counterpoint, 1998, p. 293
18. Ibid.
19. Ibid.
20. Ibid.
21. Blumenthal, *The Invisible Wall*, p. 289
22. Werner T. Angress, "The German Army's Judenzahlung of 1916," Leo Baeck Institute, Vol. 23, 1978, p. 119

not on the battlefields. The minister, in response, agreed to launch a Jewish census to ascertain a figure. The government, although not initiating the count, permitted it to take place, thereby, giving validation to the growing chorus of anti-Semitism within Germany.

The results were not made public, ostensibly to "spare Jewish feelings." The truth is that the census disproved the accusations: eighty percent had actually served on the front lines.[23]

The Jew count was a humiliating blow; especially to the thousands of young German Jewish men who were fighting and dying on the front lines. Many saw the census as a betrayal. One soldier, Julius Marx exclaimed, "So this is why we are risking our necks for this country."[24] Jewish organizations sent numerous protests to the government and received a reply justifying the census, declaring they were only to set the record straight.

When prominent German Jewish banker Max Warburg tried to convince the war ministry to reveal their own findings which would vindicate the claims of the Jews, they leaked some of their findings to a well-known anti-Semitic demagogue who published a distorted report.[25]

As the war continued, and more Germans died on the battlefields without victory in sight, the anti-Semitic charges increased. The seeds of the hatred from which Nazism would eventually spring were germinating. Some noticed these developments. In October, 1917, the Central Association of German Citizens of the Jewish Faith newspaper ominously stated, "We Jews are in for a war, after the war."[26] Ferdinand Avenarius the publisher of the highbrow magazine *Kunstwart*, warned a Jewish friend during the war that the Jews did not even begin to surmise the rage that was "boiling deep within the people."[27]

To add to the blow of the Jew Count, many Germans spread additional propaganda accusing the Jews of betraying Germany during

---

23. Amos Elan, *The Pity of it All*, p. 338
24. Ibid. p. 339
25. Ibid. p. 340
26. The weekly journal, "Variety," October, 1917
27. Elan, *The Pity of it All*, p. 338

the war. In one example, a pseudo anonymous author known as Otto Armin released a fictitious wartime account of the Jews in 1919, which imputed their loyalty. His figures slandered the Jews by stating that 62,000 Jews served in the armed forces, 35,000 served behind the front lines and only 27,000 ever saw action on the field.[28] There were also other accounts, which falsified the number of Jews in active duty. Such false accounts also contributed to the rise of anti-Semitism.

To ensure that the record be set straight, between 1917 and 1921, a census was taken by the main Jewish organizations of Germany under the direction of the Berlin State Statistical Office which after much effort came up with the following results. Of the 600,000 Jews living in Germany in 1914, 100,000 served during the war in the Army, Navy, or Colonial Troops, and 12,000 were killed in action.[29] The anti-Semites however, were uninterested in their findings.

German Jewry was aghast, but most did not realize that it was only the beginning of an avalanche of hate whose intensity would defy their worst nightmares with the eventual rise of Nazi Germany.

Great Britain

Across the English Channel, expressions of Jewish support for British war efforts were not so different. At the beginning of the war, an editorial in the London Jewish Chronicle placed the blame for the war at the doorstep of Germany. "Great Britain is engaged in a monumental struggle for life and death as a nation, a struggle that was none of her seeking and that was forced upon her."[30] The Jewish Chronicle displayed a banner outside its office which read, "ENGLAND HAS BEEN ALL SHE COULD BE TO THE JEWS, JEWS WILL BE ALL THEY CAN BE TO ENGLAND."[31]

Before the draft was imposed in 1916, ten thousand British Jews

---

28. *The Jews of Germany*, p. 243

29. "Die Judischen Gefallen, A Roll of Honor Commemorating the 12,000 German Jews who died for Their Fatherland in World War One," http:/www.GermanJewishSoldiers.com/introduction.php. Duetsche Judische Soldaten, Volksbund Kreigsgraberfursorge.(Federation of German Jewish Soldiers Website)

30. *London Jewish Chronicle*, August 7, 1914, p. 5, and *LJC*, August 21, 1914, p. 11

31. *LJC*, Ibid.

had already volunteered. This was an impressive number, considering that the total number of British Jewry was not so high.

A full page announcement was placed in The Jewish World of London, on January 12, 1916, calling on British Jewish men to enlist. The ad stated, "THERE MUST BE NO JEWISH SLACKERS."[32]

Rabbi Moses Gaster, of the Bevis Marks Synagogue also composed a prayer for the armed forces of Great Britain which contained the following lines:

> Contend for us, judge our cause, fight our battles, and destroy all those who rise up against us for evil, confound their councils, and confuse their plans. In Thy great mercy, protect those who with good courage go out to face the danger of death. Command Thou help for us against the adversary. May the land soon have rest from war.[33]

Among "all those" were the hundreds of thousands of Jewish troops fighting for the Central Powers.

British citizen Chaim Weizmann, a chemist and emerging Zionist leader, developed a method of producing acetone, a potato based raw material that could be used to make explosives at a time when the badly needed material was in short supply.[34]

A Jewish officer in the British army, Colonel Alfred Stern, helped develop the tank as a weapon. This accomplishment merited his knighting by King George V.[35]

Following the introduction of conscription in Great Britain in May, 1916, the number of Jews serving swelled to 41,500.[36]

France

In France, on August 3, 1914, a proclamation by the "Federation

---

32. *The Jewish World*, January 12, 1916, p. 23

33. *LJC*, October 9, 1914, p. 16

34. www.weizmann.ac.il

35. Martin Gilbert, p. 69

36. V.D. Lipman, *A History of the Jews in England Since 1858*, Leicester University Press, 1990, p. 143

of Jewish Societies" responded to Jewish immigrants who were reluctant to join the war cause due to the alliance of the Entente with
Russia on account of its anti-Semitic policies. It stated that, "While
the whole of the French people rises as one man to the defense of
the fatherland, shall we stand with our arms folded? No, if we are
not yet Frenchmen in law, we are so in heart and soul."[37]

In one show of support of the war effort by French Jews, over
two thousand took part in a patriotic demonstration. The crowd
consisted mostly of Jewish immigrants who carried French, English,
Russian, and Belgium flags, as well as banners with French and Yiddish inscriptions appealing to the Jews to come to the assistance of
France. The demonstrators marched through the streets singing
the French National Anthem and shouting "A Berlin [to Berlin]
Christians everywhere greeted the Jewish procession with great enthusiasm."[38]

Russia

Russian Jews participated in patriotic rallies. One such event occurred in the city of Tiflis (Kavkas), after the morning services. One
Saturday, the Jews marched as a group to the governor-general's
palace and held a patriotic demonstration.[39]

Despite the history of persecution of Russian Jewry and the severe pogroms that had been perpetrated in prior decades, there were
many pronouncements of loyalty.

An appeal from Jews in Vilna, one of many such appeals stated,

> Our dear fatherland – the great Russia – has been called to a
> dreadful, bloody battle; a merciless struggle for the integrity
> and greatness of Russia is underway. All the faithful sons of the
> fatherland have risen as one, to protect the fatherland from
> invasion by enemies. And our brothers in faith – the Jews – have

---

37. Quoted from, Paula Hyman, *From Dreyfus to Vichy: The Remaking of French Jewry*, Columbia University Press, New York, 1979, p. 56
38. *LJC*, August 21, 1914, p. 13
39. *The Canadian Jewish Chronicle*, August 21, 1914, Page 1

proved willing throughout the Russian Empire to perform their civic duty, and many have voluntarily joined the ranks of the army which has set off to the field of battle.[40]

In the first edition after the declaration of war, the Russian Jewish (press) organ *Novy Voskhod* stated: "We were born and have grown up in Russia, the ashes of our ancestors rest here. We, the Russian Jews, are inextricably bound to Russia, and our brothers, banished across the ocean by an evil fate, lovingly cherish memories of Russia all their lives. The keepers of the covenants of our fathers, the nucleus of world Jewry, we, the Russian Jews, are at the same time inalienably bound to the country in which we have lived for hundreds of years already and from which nothing – neither persecution nor victimization – is capable of separating us. At this historical moment, when our motherland is threatened by foreign invasion, when brute force has taken up arms against the supreme ideals of humanity, Russian Jewry will courageously enter the battlefield and perform its sacred duty."[41]

In an historical session of the State Duma (parliament) at the beginning of the war, member of parliament, N.M. Friedman, stated that "in the great storm which has raised all the tribes and peoples of Russia, the Jews are entering the battlefield shoulder to shoulder with all its people, that no forces can detach the Jews from their motherland – Russia, from the land with which they are bound by century-long bonds," and that "in defense of their motherland from foreign invasion, Jews are acting not only from duty of conscience, but from a feeling of deep loyalty towards Russia. . . ."[42]

Many Russian Jews lived with hope that the Russian Czar would finally grant them emancipation. A report by the Paris correspondent Exchange Telegraph Company stated that the Czar would sign a proclamation granting the Jews in his dominions equal civil and

---

40. Simon Dubnov, *The Black Book of Russian Jewry*, Yevreiskaya Starina, (Jewish Antiquities) Jewish Historical Ethnographic Society, Volume 10, St. Petersburg, 1918, p. 199
   41. Ibid. p. 200
   42. Ibid. p. 202

political rights with the other subjects. Such rumors heightened the enthusiasm among some Russian Jews.[43] Many believed that freedom was forthcoming.

Yet, despite the public demonstrations in support, there was great concern over the war's outcome and how it would impact the lives of the recruits and the entire community. Many viewed the emergence of war with foreboding concern, as a harbinger of bad news. (They saw troubled times ahead, but nonetheless would not defy the Russian Czar and answered the call to arms.)

In March, 1917 with the fall of the Czar, a new era was heralded by some Russian Jews. Yet, the revolution did not bring democracy and soon ushered in a dark era of Communist tyranny.

Austria-Hungary

Jews of the Austro-Hungarian Empire also ardently showed their support. Austrian Jews also viewed the war as a means of defeating Russia and liberating its Jewish community from Czarist persecution. Russia, the only foe which Austria-Hungary was fighting directly, was deemed an arch enemy of the Jews for the pogroms inflicted upon Russian Jews over the prior decades.

Moritz Fruhling, who later published several books on Jews in the war, asserted that Jewish soldiers, "must take revenge for all of the atrocities committed against our brothers, must make expiation of our raped and murdered sisters."[44]

In a telegram to its American brother organization, the Austrian B'nai B'rith declared that the war was a "battle of freedom against slavery. . . . a battle on behalf of the millions of our horribly oppressed and persecuted co-religionists."[45]

In addition, the Jewish Press coupled patriotism with the hope that Jewish valor on the battlefield would help them achieve full

---

43. *The Canadian Jewish Chronicle*, August 21, 1914, p. 1

44. P. Marsha I. Rozenblit, *Reconstructing a National Identity: The Jews of Hapsburg Austria During World War I*, Oxford University Press, 2001, p. 45 quoted from, OW, 7 August, 1914, pp. 547–548

45. Ibid. p. 45, quoted from Zweimonats-Bericht . . . der . . . B'nai B'rith, vol. 17, #4 (1914) p. 27

emancipation. The Austrian Israelite Union newspaper described the Jews as most loyal and ready to sacrifice and give their lives for the Fatherland. At the same time, they expected that "The blood of our sons dedicated to the fatherland" would entitle the Jews to "full undiminished equality."[46] While Emperor Franz Joseph had granted the Jews emancipation decades earlier, there were limitations and anti-Semitism persisted within the empire.

The United States

Most Jews in America like the US population at large initially opposed participation in the war and therefore supported neutrality. However, there was also a particular motive for their opposition, in that the Entente included Russia. Jewish socialists in New York City, such as the editor of the Daily (Yiddish) Forward Abraham Cahan and labor leader Samuel Untermeyer, were reluctant to support an alliance with the oppressive Czar whose anti-Semitic and general economic policies they abhorred. The socialist Cahan wrote, "Convinced in the interests of general progress and for Jews specifically a Russian defeat would be fortunate. . . . that it would be fortunate for all of Europe and the whole Jewish population if Germany would take all of Poland and also Lithuania from Russia."[47]

Jewish Trade Unions in New York and Chicago held meetings and rallies to "keep our country from being dragged into the war." An AFL (American Federation of Labor) rally on April 15, 1915 protested arms production, which were sent to the allies, namely the British, opposing any kind of support for the Entente. It was supported by the powerful I.L.G.W.U. (International Ladies Garment Workers Union) and the Ladies Waist Makers Union. Many synagogues also issued resolutions that called for peace.[48]

On August 3, 1914, the Orthodox Morgen Journal stated that

---

46. Ibid. p. 44 quoted from MONOIU, July-August, 1914, pp. 1–2

47. Abraham Cahan in *The Forward*. December 10, 1914, p. 18

48. *Morgen Journal*, August 3, 1914, quoted from Morris Schappes, *Jewish Life*, Vol. 19, February, 1955, "World War I and the Jewish Masses," p. 18

"France will get what she deserved for this alliance."[49] On September 9, the Morgen Journal regretted that England might be defeated, but if it were, "it will only be a sign that there is historical justice."[50]

Everything Changes

US Congressman from New York, Meyer London, wrote in the New York Tribune on March 10, 1917, that if the US entered the war, American socialists would follow the lead of European socialists and support their government.[51]

With the fall of the Russian Czar in March, 1917, and the American Declaration of war one month later, positions within the Jewish community changed to one of support for the war effort.

In Great Britain, likewise, recent Jewish immigrants largely did not support a war which would side them with their former oppressors, Czarist Russia. As non-citizens they were not subject to the draft, and generally avoided volunteering. To other British Jews, they were a source of embarrassment.

Noted Jewish Thinkers Respond

In Germany, due to the heightened war fervor and also possible repercussions against those who spoke out amid an environment of censorship, there was limited Jewish opposition. However, there were some Jewish intellectuals who expressed opposition. Albert Einstein refused to sign a manifesto justifying the German invasion of Belgium at the beginning of the war. Einstein viewed the war as "madness."[52] He composed his own manifesto against the war which only three academic colleagues signed. Left wing writer and satirist, Kurt Tucholsky, wrote of the horrors of the war. German socialist and co-founder of the Sparticist league, the Marxist revolutionary

---

49. Ibid. p. 17
50. Ibid. p. 18
51. Ibid. p. 19
52. Rivka Horwitz, *Voices of Opposition to the First World War Among Jewish Thinkers*, Leo Baeck Institute, Vol. 33, January, 1988, p. 238

movement, Karl Liebnecht, was known for his opposition to World War One for which he spent two and a half years in prison for participating in an anti-war protest on June 1, 1916. The Socialist writer, Gustav Landauer, who rejected the optimism of others, believed there was no moral justification for the war and that no good would come from it.

The future Judaic studies scholar Gershom Scholem was convinced that there was a contradiction between Jewish interests and military service for Germany. He believed that German Jews were living in a world of self-deception, hoping for integration in Germany, while disregarding anti-Semitism which is largely downplayed. He wrote, "This capacity for self-deception is one of the most important and dismal aspects of the German Jewish relationship."[53] Scholem, who was thrown out of his home by his father for defending his brother who was court marshaled for attending an anti-war rally in full uniform, was already alarmed at the anti-Semitic writings circulated in Germany.[54] Unlike, Scholem, who feigned insanity to avoid the draft, most Jews with reservations and eligible for the draft served nonetheless out of loyalty to Germany. Two such individuals were the Jewish philosopher Franz Rosenzweig and the aforementioned Gustav Landauer.[55] Over time, as the war continued and the casualties mounted, voices of opposition were more commonly heard.

Within the Austro-Hungarian Empire, in a small Galitzian town, the outbreak of the war was received not much differently from other small Jewish villages within Europe. War brings upheaval and sufferings. Its outcome is unpredictable. The novelist Manes Sperber remembered his father stating that "For us this war is a terrible disaster." "Why a disaster?" Someone asked, "Our Kaiser will be victorious and the Czar will be defeated and will never oppress his subjects again." He replied, "For us every war is a disaster, no one in this room can be sure of his survival."[56]

---

53. Gershom Scholem, *From Berlin to Jerusalem: Memoirs of My Youth*, Translated from the German by Harry Zohn, Schocken Books, New York, 1980, p. 26

54. Rivka Horwitz, *Voices of Opposition to the First World War Among Jewish Thinkers*, Leo Baeck Institute, Vol. 33, January, 1988, p.257

55. Ibid. 259

56. Manes Sperber, *All das Vernangene*, Fisher, Vienna, 1983, p. 121

From the city of Warsaw, Poland, the father of the Yiddish author Isaac Bashevis Singer, initially greeted news of the outbreak of the First World War gleefully with the expectation that the greatest enemies of the Jews, the dreaded Cossacks would be swiftly defeated by the Germans. Singer wrote, "Running home from the Radzymin study house, my father announced that he had heard the war would be over in two weeks. 'They have cannons that can kill a thousand Cossacks at one blow.'"[57] But that optimism would soon turn to dread as Eastern European Jewry faced devastation.

The historian Jacob Katz wrote about his early youth in the Hungarian town of Magyargencs, following the Russian invasion of Galicia in 1914. At the time he was ten years old. He recalls the ominous tone.

> On Sabbath eve, the first of August 1914, the town crier's drum resounded in the middle of the night. This official would pass through the village street beating his drum and pause at the given spot; once all had assembled, he would read out whatever announcement the government wished to bring to the public. . . . The timing of these events had a peculiar significance, as one deeply etched upon my memory. That particular Shabbat was Shabbat Chazzon, in which the first chapter of the book of Isaiah was read in the Synagogue to herald the approach of the Ninth of Av, the anniversary of the destruction of the Temple.[58]

Jewish Statehood

Amid the hardships that ensued during this era which was also imbued with the spirit of nationalism and minority rights, increasing attention was focused upon the question of Jewish rights to their ancient homeland. Jewish repatriation to the Land of Israel became a matter of heightened concern in the Jewish world and among many

---

57. Isaac Bashevis Singer, *In My Father's Court*, Farrar, Strauss, and Giroux, New York, 1991, p. 229

58. Jacob Katz, *With My Own Eyes: The Autobiography of an Historian*, The Tauber Institute for the Study of European Jewry, 1995, p. 19

non-Jewish leaders as well. The First World War was a time of horror for the Jews and also a time which signaled the emergence of the movement for Jewish independence.

In a world of chaos, desperation, and anti-Semitic persecution, the dream of Jewish Statehood gained support within world Jewry. In the very early stages of the war, there was hope that Turkey whose empire extended over the Land of Israel would offer independence to the Jews, especially in light of the military advances of their ally, Germany, into Poland, where so many Jews resided. But the Turks showed no such interest. Rather, they acted in opposition to those ends by treating the Jews of Palestine with a very heavy hand.[59] Only outside intervention mainly from the Americans, then a neutral party, prevented the worsening of an already dire situation.

The Situation in Palestine

The Jews of Palestine had suffered to the extent where the Jewish community itself appeared in danger. Over half its Jewish population was lost to starvation, disease, expulsion, and flight. Of the estimated 60,000 Jews of Jerusalem in 1914, only 23,000 remained by the end of the war.[60]

Through the publication of the Balfour Declaration, a statement by the British government recognizing Jewish Statehood on November 2, 1917, as the British were completing the conquest of Palestine from the Turks, Jewish statehood, appeared to be forthcoming, but not as soon as hoped.

Many Jews had hoped that the era preceding the war would bring them closer to dreams of emancipation. Others, generally, the more traditional, did not consider such notions, accepting their status as outsiders among the nations.

---

59. The term "Palestine" was a commonly used reference to the Land of Israel since ancient Greece to the British Mandate of Palestine in the 20th century. Palestine was a land within empires where Jews, Christians, and Muslims resided. It does not apply to the currently used reference as an Arab entity seeking national independence.

60. Vladimir Jabotinsky, *The Story of the Jewish Legion*, Bernard Ackerman, New York, 1945, p. 119

In an era of nationalism, some Jews, namely the Zionists, saw Jewish nationalism as a solution to the ills of anti-Semitism, with the hope that as a nation they would find acceptance among other nations.

The war did significantly advance the goal of Jewish Statehood, leading to its eventual creation.

Time of Warning

In 1913, the following poem penned by the writer Zalman Schneur, entitled "The Middle Ages Draw Near," foresaw the modern day catastrophe emerging from the turbulence of war and the new post '"enlightenment" world in which hatred and anti-Semitism was on the rise. He foresaw the horrors which awaited European Jewry during this ill-fated era, and exhorted his fellow Jews to see the imminent dangers and heed the warning.

> Mighty is the approaching winter
> for summer tarried in the land
> The middle ages draw near!
> Like a cloud in the distance
> Open wide your eyes and ears, ancient people!
> The wheel is . . . the turning wheel:
> And a wild wind before it.[61]

---

61. *Modern Hebrew Poetry, A Bilingual Anthology*, Edited and Translated by Ruth Finer Mintz, University of California Press, Berkley, AC, pp. 91,92

Chapter 2

The Germans Advance East into Poland

Our pursuers were swifter than eagles in the sky:
they chased us in the mountains,
and ambushed us in the streets.[62]

O n August 3, 1914, Russian forces launched an attack against Germany and following their initial advances, they were routed at Mazurian Lakes. Surviving Russian forces retreated as the German advance into Poland began.

One of the first cities over the Polish border occupied by German troops was Kalisch, which like other cities near the border faced the weight and fury of the German army. The town was virtually leveled and its citizens faced violence and mayhem.

Jewish communities lay in the path of the German onslaught and were victims of the German advance, as were local Poles.

There were acts of violence perpetrated against the Jews by the Germans. The Anglo Jewish press was quick to point out the crimes of the German enemy against Jews. While there were some German troops who did act against the Jews, they were not specifically targeted by the Germans as a matter of policy.

Western European journals regularly reported misconduct by the German army. So too, the Jewish media in Great Britain and France highlighted German misconduct against the Jews. At the beginning of the war, the London Jewish Chronicle published a weekly segment entitled, "German Atrocities," which contained reports of atrocities committed against Jews. On August 28, 1914 the London Jewish

---

62. Lamentations 4:19

Chronicle reported that German troops executed Jewish hostages in Kalish.[63] At Konin (near Kalish) the Germans took fifteen Jews as hostages. According to the story, the German Commander, named Von Launitz, threatened to kill five of the hostages in the event of any disobedience on the part of the local population.[64] At another town, Dzevitza, four Jews were shot by the Germans after being accused of informing the enemy's commander that there were no Russian troops in the neighborhood, when according to German claims, they actually were there. At the town of Dzevitza, the rabbi of the town had issued an urgent appeal on behalf of hundreds of local Jews whose houses and property had been burned by the Germans.[65] At Radom, also near the German Polish border there were similar reports. There, the Germans reportedly shot six members of a Jewish family named Rottenberg (including a mother and two daughters) who they accused of warning the Cossacks of the presence of Germans in the town.[66]

These instances reflected upon the horrors of war and the anti-Semitism of individuals in the German army.

Many Jews in the path of the German advance fled, marking the beginnings of the massive flight of Jewish refugees during the war.

Despite the brutality of the German invasion, many German Jewish troops saw the moment as one of opportunity. For some, the invasion was a battle for liberation. By fighting oppressive Russia, they considered themselves to be battling on behalf of Russian Jewry. The battle cry for some invading German Jewish soldiers was "Revenge for Kishinev" referring to the anti-Jewish atrocities perpetrated in the 1904 Kishinev massacres.

The Germans marched into Lodz in early December, 1914, singing a song ridiculing a Russian commander who had organized a pogrom before withdrawing from the city. The song composed in

---

63. *LJC*, October 2, 1914, p. 11
64. *LJC*, Ibid.
65. *LJC*, October 9, 1914, p. 11
66. *LJC*, October 2, 1914, p. 15

1861 stated, "Christians and Jews are violent foes. But they're united when it comes to halting the Russians."[67]

The German invasion would not free the Jews of their suffering. With the withdrawals of Russian forces through Poland, Jews would be maligned and falsely blamed by Russians and local Poles of consorting with the enemy although hundreds of thousands of Russian Jews were fighting in the Russian army. Whatever quiet Polish Jewry (under Czarist Russian occupation since the late 18th century) had known, came to an end. Russians forces retreating eastward perpetrated devastating attacks against Jewish communities causing tens of thousands of Jews to flee for their lives as refugees. Russian commanders also issued expulsion orders against Jewish communities in their path from the beginning of the Russian retreat. The first expulsion order was issued on August 11 from the town of Khotin.

Likewise in the land of Galitzia to the south of Poland, Jews would very soon face a massive wave of persecution at the hands of the Russian forces.

Just one year before the outbreak of war, the Russian masses were whipped into a fury over the bogus charges of ritual murder leveled against Mendel Beilis. The infamous trial, rife with anti-Semitic vitriol was a rallying call for Russia's Jew baiters and haters. The Beilis case was a preamble of the Anti-Semitic storm to follow.

Russian Spy Mania

It was the product of hatred; the character assassination of an entire people. It was also a means of deflecting blame from the failures of the Russian military to the Jews. As Russian forces began their retreats, accusations of treason almost immediately surfaced against the Jews of Poland who would soon face a deluge of charges claiming the Jews assisted the Germans and spied for them. Bizarre and outrageous as they were, these claims were readily accepted especially among military personnel. Some included firing upon Russian

---

67. Edited by Rafael Patai, Herzl Yearbook, Herzl Press, Vol. 7, January, 1971, "The Komitee fur Den Osten and Zionism" (The Committee for the East and Zionism), p. 203

troops, signaling the enemy, placing mines and smuggling money. The Jews were frequently accused of shipping large sums of rubles to Germany; Sending secret messages, or receiving massive amounts of gold in return.

Jews were accused of digging tunnels miles long into enemy lines.[68] Others reported that Jews directed enemy fire from balloons, and provided the Austrians with secret information, luring the Russians into traps. Some even stated that Jews burned their own homes before fleeing westward in the direction of the Germans.[69] Other accusations included supplying the enemy with gold and foodstuffs. According to another, the innards of dead poultry were stuffed with gold, and the dead poultry was sent to Germany.[70] Tales emerged about the gold exported abroad by the Jews in a coffin. Another tale emerged about a Jew on a white horse riding ahead of the troops and giving signals to the enemy.[71] One of the most common accusations was that Jews were communicating with the enemy by hand held phones.[72] In one example, on the Sabbath, the police entered the synagogue in a village and ordered that the Torah Scrolls be removed so they could search for secret telephones.[73]

Russian soldiers hanged a man from a tree for allegedly signaling to the enemy. He was returning home but he first wanted to climb on a tree just to check if his house was still intact.[74]

At a Jewish funeral in Warsaw, the tale was that a coffin examined by the authorities was found to contain twenty-five million rubles in gold, which it was thought the Jews kept for the invading Germans.[75]

The Russian army newspaper, the *Russky Invalide* charged that

---

68. Alexander Victor Prusin, *Nationalizing a Borderland*, University of Alabama Press, Tuscaloosa, ALA, 2005, p. 27

69. Ibid.

70. Dubnov, *Black Book*, p. 210

71. Ibid.

72. *LJC*, February 19, 1915, p. 21, "The soldiers thought that they were communicating with the enemy through a wireless telephone."

73. *New York Times*, February 4, 1915, p. 15

74. Joachim Neugroshel, *The Enemy at His Pleasure: A Journey Through the Hebrew Pale Settlement During World War One*, Holt/Metropolitan, New York, 2003, p. 116

75. *B'nai B'rith News*, November, 1914, p. 6

before the war, the German government intentionally impoverished the Jews of Posen and East Prussia on the Polish German border and subsequently subsidized them to settle in large numbers in Russian Poland in order to act as spies. The paper accused the Jews of treachery and expressed the opinion that after the war among the military reforms, the Jews will have to be cleared from the frontier.[76]

Other anti-Semitic journals picked up this information and reproduced the charges. Anti-Semitism had become commonplace in the Russian military.

The policy was one of expulsion of Jews near the war zones. It was enacted partly because of a scorched earth policy where nothing would be left for the pursuing Germans and also as a means to persecute the Jewish population. By libeling the Jews, leaders of the Russian military had found a convenient scapegoat for their military failures. They could blame the Jews and falsely accuse them of consorting with the Germans.

Spoken Yiddish was also prohibited by the Russian authorities out of fear of contact between Jews and Germans, due to the similarities between German and Yiddish.

There were efforts by Jews and non-Jews to refute the propaganda. In one example, the chief Rabbi of Warsaw along with other leaders sent a telegraph to the leading newspaper, *Novoe Vremya* which refused to publish the message.[77] Even if an occasional retraction would be granted, the story was already disseminated and the damage was done.

By publishing charges of treason in state sponsored newspapers, incitement and violence against the Jews intensified. Violence was perpetrated by Cossacks, and sometimes by members of the Russian military and Poles seeking to curry favor with the Russian army.

Expulsions

The slander was a pretext for the forced expulsions that soon followed. It was the outcome of the hate propaganda against the Jews.

---

76. With the abolition of the Pale Settlement following the expulsions.
77. American Jewish Committee, *Jews in the Eastern War Zone*, p. 51

The justification being that the Jews were perceived (falsely) as a security threat. The following are some of the earliest expulsions.

In early August, 1914, in Yanovtse (Radom Governorate), the entire Jewish population was expelled.[78] In the village of Ryk (Radom Governorate near the Polish border), the Jewish population of the trading quarter was expelled twice: on August 27 and September 25.[79] On September 23, 1914, on the orders of the commandant of the Ivangorod Fortress, the entire Jewish population was expelled in 24 hours' notice from Novaya Aleksandria (Lublin Governorate). In the village of Irena (Lublin Governorate), on September 28, 1914, all the Jews were expelled.[80] In the village of Pyasechno (Warsaw Governorate), on October 7, 1914, the entire Jewish population was expelled.[81] In Grodzisk (Warsaw Governorate), on October 14, 1914, at 11:00 am, the Jews were ordered to leave the town by the evening. Around 4,000 were expelled on that day, which included around 300 families of army reservists. At the start of November, they were permitted to return, but on January 25, 1915, another order was issued on their expulsion within a period of 2 days.[82] In the village of Kernozya (Warsaw Governorate), on November 7, 1914, the entire population of the town, Poles and Jews left. After 2–3 days, the Poles returned. The Jews were not permitted to do so.[83]

In secret and with dread, like thieves in the night, refugees showed up at the homes of their relatives and friends. After staying a few days and nights in secret, the pleas and requests to the authorities began stating that the danger of the war was the reason for the flight and that the confiscation of property and the presence of relatives were the reasons for their illegally entry. A permit to reside at that location was therefore being requested. Thus temporary permits were issued for some weeks and even months.[84]

---

78. Dubnov, *Black Book of Russian Jewry*, p. 215
79. Ibid.
80. Ibid.
81. Ibid.
82. Ibid.
83. Ibid.
84. Graubart, *Sefer Zikaron*, p. 264 Quoted from the journal, HaIvri, 'HaTalot Hayehudim' (Trevails of the Jews in the Great War) by M. Katz.

Mass Expulsion

The expulsions soon became more organized, and better coordinated on a massive scale. On January 25, 1915, with the Russian army continuing to retreat, the first mass expulsion was enacted. Over one hundred thousand Jews were abruptly forced from their homes by decree.[85]

The expulsion order by senior military authorities was issued for more than forty settlements in the Warsaw region. The two individuals most responsible for the expulsions were the commander of the military, General Nikolai Nikolovich, the uncle of the Czar and the Chief of Staff General Nikolai Yanushkavich, who was known for his enmity towards the Jews.

The term expulsion does not adequately describe the trauma inflicted upon the victims.

With such rapid mass expulsions of masses of people from their homes in the winter, usually with the absence of horses and carts, it was a scene of the horrors of travelling on foot with the sick and with children, facing hunger, and sometimes death under the open skies.

In addition to serving in the army, many able bodied men, mainly of working age had emigrated from Russia over recent years. For the most part, it was women, children, and the elderly who faced expulsion.

The French ambassador to Russia, Maurice Paleologue, described the tragic events.

> After a short respite the expulsions have begun again in the most summary, hasty, and brutal manner. . . . Everywhere the process of departure has been marked by scenes of violence and pillage under the complacent eyes of the authorities. Hundreds of thousands of these poor people have been wandering over the snows, driven like cattle by platoons of Cossacks, abandoned in the great distress and the stations, camping in the open, round the towns, and dying of hunger, wariness and cold.[86]

---

85. Dubnov, *Black Book of Russian Jewry*, p. 218
86. Maurice Paleologue: *An Ambassador's Memoirs*, Translated by F.A. Holt,

Exiles converged upon Warsaw from all directions by rail, by road, or by country roads. Over 80,000 people gathered in Warsaw alone. They were physically broken, haggard, morally stunned, accompanied by the destruction of property. Violence was perpetrated against them and against their honor, having turned in part from self-sufficient people into beggars.

The expulsions were often accompanied by pogroms.

The New York Times quoted a German rabbi at the front describing conditions facing Jewry.

> My heart is wrung when I see and hear what terrible crimes of violence have been executed upon Jews by the Russians in the course of the present war and are still being carried out. The pogroms of former days are nothing compared to the savage destruction of Jewish homes and Jewish lives, that sweeps forward and backward, like a threatening shadow, with the coming and going of the Russian hosts throughout Poland. So far, pogroms have been carried on in more than 215 places and no end to this terror is in sight.[87]

The article continued,

> In Ostrowisc, the Cossacks demanded the surrender of the Rabbi, Zaddik Kalischer, who was to be hanged on the charge of favoring the Austrians. As a matter of fact, he together with the Polish Priest had gone forward to meet the Austro-German troops, even as he had gone forward earlier to meet the Russians in order to beg that the inhabitants of the place be treated humanely. Inasmuch as the rabbi concealed himself, the Cossacks waited for the approaching Yom Kippur, and surrounded the synagogue, in order to arrest the rabbi there. Just as they were on the point of bursting into the house of prayer the Germans

87. *New York Times*, February 4, 1915, "Tells of Russians' Murder of Jews" p.15

marched into Ostrowisc and the Russians fled after first destroying the house and grounds of the rabbi.[88]

In Zyrardow, Prushkow, Bialobrzeg, Ivangorod, Grodzisk, Skiernewisc, and many other places, all the Jews were expelled. The Jews of Grodzisk wanted to go toward Warsaw, and begged for permission, through a deputation. The General ordered them to go to the left bank of the Vistula, and when they replied that that was the same as ordering them to go into the Vestula, he replied, cynically: 'That would be best of all.[89]

In Bachawa [Government of Lublin] 78 Jews were hanged on one day in October on charges of espionage.[90]

In Kramostow [Government of Lublin] many houses were burned to the ground, and the Jews (200 families) were annihilated. They consisted mostly of women and children.[91]

In Lodz, 15,000 small tradesmen were robbed of their property and made beggars.[92]

Following the expulsions of January 25, there was a brief lull. The impact and negative international reactions to the persecutions might have brought about the short pause in the mass expulsions, and then they would resume with even greater brutality less than two months later.

The Russian Advance into Galitzia

Galitzia is a territory in Eastern Europe to the South of Poland, to the West of Ukraine and North of Hungary and Austria. The over one million Jews of Galitzia lived under the Austro-Hungarian empire whose leader, Emperor Franz Joseph had granted emancipation to the Jews twenty years earlier.

The Russians attacked Galitzia on August 18 since they consid-

---

88. Ibid.
89. Ibid.
90. Ibid.
91. Ibid.
92. Ibid.

ered it part of the Russian Empire, and because of commitments to their alliance with France and Great Britain. The first battle over Galitzia would be a very costly Russian victory over Austrian forces. On September 2, 1914, Russian forces successfully attacked the city of Lemburg (Lvov). By September 11, Eastern Galitzia was under Russian control. On September 15, the Russians succeeded in capturing the nearby fortress city of Przemysl, a key location. Jews by the tens of thousands began to flee westward. On June 3, 1915, the Austrian-Hungarians retook Przemysl.

The following is the text of the expulsion decree of Jews from Przemysl following the Russian capture. As other expulsion decrees at the time, expulsions were swift and the threatened repercussions for non-compliance were severe.

"To the Jewish Implementation Committee: By the orders of the commander of the fortress of Przemysl, I am giving notification that the Jews living in and around Przemysl must exit as quickly as possible. To assist the evacuation, I have established a committee made up of Jews. Railroad trains will be available to the departing Jewish inhabitants. If the Jews do not leave willingly and if they refuse to implement the directives set forth by the committee, I will be forced to utilize severe measures; as a company of Cossacks will expeditiously implement the evacuation, and the rebellious Jews can only blame themselves." "Administrator of the Przemysl district: Guard Corporal Kiriakov."[93]

The expulsion had taken place on the Sabbath. On Friday evening, in synagogue, where the Jews prayed for the last time, their bitter wailing was indescribable. After the prayers, the synagogue was closed down.[94]

Urging on anti-Jewish measures was the chief of staff of the Russian army, General Yanushkevich, again leveling accusations that Jews were enemies of Russia as he sought severe measures against Galitzian Jewry. The military in Galitzia as in Poland and Russia, was mainly responsible for the anti-Jewish enactments.

---

93. Shalom Ansky, *Churban HaYeudim, B'Polin, Galitzia, Uv'Bukovina*, Shtieble Publishing, Tel Aviv, 1929, p. 99
94. Ibid. based upon a testimony by a physician, Dr. Shapiro.

By December, 1914, due to the outbreak of pogroms in the area, more than forty thousand Jews from the countryside had fled northwards to the city of Lvov.[95] Most Jews fled southward to other cities as well.

Hostage Taking

Soon after Przemysl, the Russian high command proceeded to expel the Jews of Lvov. In early January (1915), a notice was pasted up in Polish and German on all the streets of Lvov and other Galitzian towns, "The experience of the current war has identified the clear hostility towards us of the Jews of Poland, Galitzia and Bukovina." The notice continued, "So as to free our troops from spying, in which the Jews are engaged on the entire front, the Commander in Chief has prohibited the Jews from being present in the region of the Army and . . . by way of identifying spying by Jews, has ordered that hostages be taken, who will be punished (execution by hanging) . . . for each Jewish spy caught, two hostages will be accountable."[96]

As a most sinister means of ensuring compliance with orders, hostages were taken which was often accompanied by an unusual kind of bargaining. First and foremost, the wealthiest individuals were taken hostage; they were then released for a certain ransom and in their place a second-priority set of people were often taken who were also then released for a ransom, and in their place a third-priority set of people were taken. This practice was also frequent on the Russian front as well.

Shalom Ansky

Jewish writer, ethnographer and activist, Shlomo Zanvel Rappaport, known by his pen name, Shalom Ansky, was best known for his play, the *Dybbuk*. When the news of the persecutions in Galitzia became clear, Anski decided that he would to the best of his ability aid the beleaguered Jews there and in neighboring Poland. His mission was

---

95. Prusin, *Nationalizing a Borderland*, p. 42
96. Dubnov, *Black Book of Russian Jewry*, p. 212

to report on their suffering and raise and distribute funds among the desperate. In late 1914, Ansky accompanied Russian forces into Galitzia and Poland on behalf of Jewish relief agencies. In his accounts on his war time experiences and the plight of Jews near the war zones in a memoir entitled, "The Jewish Calamity in Poland, Galitzia and Bukovina,"[97] Ansky presented chilling and in depth reporting on the perilous situation facing the Jews. He described what he witnessed as "one of the darkest times in the history of the Jews."[98] He wrote vivid descriptions of the destruction of Jewish life in Galitzia and Poland. He described Galitzia as a great land once with one million Jews who yesterday had enjoyed civil rights granted by Austro-Hungarian Emperor, Franz Joseph, and now faced devastation under the rule of bloodthirsty Cossacks and soldiers as if "a tribe of Israel had been cut off."[99]

Tragically, his efforts and those of others who offered assistance, while vitally important, fell far short of the enormous needs given the situation facing hundreds of thousands of Jewish refugees.

He reported the words of one Jewish soldier,

> My hands shake and my eyes fill with tears when I think of the horrors I've seen in Galicia, when I remember the horrific images that I happened to witness here in Galitzia, and the acts of cruelty committed by the Cossacks, and the soldiers. The Jews were murdered, women were violated in the streets. The hands of the elderly and of the women were cut off and they were left to die in agony.[100]
>
> Wherever the Russian army would pass, the Christians would place icons in their windows, and upon their doors. A house without icons was assumed to be Jewish, and the soldiers could damage it with impunity. When our unit passed through one village, a soldier noticed a house on top of a hill, and he

---

97. Bukavina is a region to the East of Galitzia also within the Austro-Hungarian Empire, which was also occupied by Russian troops during the war. There was a substantial Jewish community although significantly smaller than that of Galitzia.

98. Anski, *Churban Galitzia*, p. 11

99. Ibid. p. 14

100. Ibid. p. 13

notified the commander that it was probably a Jewish home. The officer had him go and have a look. A few minutes later, the soldier returned, and joyfully informed the officer that there were in fact Jews in the home. The officer ordered soldiers to approach the house. When they opened the door, they found about twenty Jews petrified with fear. The troops forced them out of the home, and the officer shouted out his order: "Slice them up! Chop them up!" I fled the home and thus did not see what happened next. I kept running until I collapsed.[101]

Cruelty knew no bounds. Ansky wrote that Cossacks would cut off the hands and feet of Jews and bury them alive.[102]

Ansky reported on many pogroms near the war zone. The Lvov pogrom which preceded the expulsion of its Jews was described by Rabbi Hoyzer, also a relief worker.

The Russians marched in without perpetrating anti-Jewish violence; an unusual happening. But soon some shooting occurred on the eve of Yom Kippur. There was a rumor that a Jewish girl had shot at the Russian military from a window and wounded or killed somebody. It was similar to the story that was spread at Brody before its destruction. A pogrom broke out. Eighteen Jews were murdered and stores were plundered. The frightened Jews did not attend synagogue for the Yom Kippur *Kol Nidrei* prayers. The hundreds of Jewish soldiers in the Czarist army went to the synagogue, but seeing it was closed, they assumed that the Russian authorities had prohibited its use. They sent a group to the then governor-general who called for the Rabbi and rebuked him for closing the Synagogues. The rabbi replied that the Jews were afraid to go outdoors and that this was not a gesture of protest over the pogroms. The governor general in response established armed patrols at all synagogues and

---

101. Ibid. p. 13
102. Ibid. p. 14

yeshivas and offered a guarantee to the Jews that there would not be another pogrom.[103]

Yom Kippur

A soldier related to Anski that on Erev Yom Kippur his unit entered a town in Galitzia. The city was in flames and partially destroyed. Only in certain spots there were still undamaged homes. No one was found in the unlit streets. It was dark as a cemetery. Suddenly, two Jews appeared. One elderly and the other young both dressed in torn and shabby coats. Upon their faces, the horrors that they experienced were evident. They also made an impression upon the non-Jewish soldiers who did not attempt to harm them. The two Jews entered an alley way and the soldier followed them. They passed through two more alley ways until they arrived at a large and old synagogue. Its windows were smashed and its doors were unhinged. The soldier followed the two Jews into the synagogue. Its interior appeared as a ruin, everything was broken. The *Aron Kodesh* (Holy Ark) was in pieces over the floor. The *Menorahs* (candelabras) were broken. The floor was covered with torn fragments of books. In the place of the *Amud*, there was a bench with a candle burning in place of the *Ner Tamid*. (Eternal flame) Other than these two Jews, an additional four were present. The elderly man stood before the bench and began to chant the *Kol Nidrei* prayer.[104]

Anski asked the solder if he tried to converse with them. The soldier looked at him and said in a low trembling voice, "I did not have the strength to speak with them. I could cry with them. So I cried."

Kiddush Levana

The *Kiddush Levana* (blessing over the moon) prayer draws a comparison between the moon, the lunar cycle and the Jewish people. Just as the appearance of the moon diminishes, and then reappears,

---

103. Ibid. p. 121
104. Ibid. p. 95

so too, the Jews from their darkest eras, facing grave dangers, will reemerge to once again shine.

Anski related an event that was reported to him by a Jew from the city of Dubnov that is tied to *Kiddush Levana*.

This Jew had arrived to the city of Redzhivilov only to find that a pogrom was taking place. The Cossacks had broken open the doors of the city and proceeded to brutalize the inhabitants. The Jews had locked themselves inside their homes. This Jew desperately seeking refuge, knocked on doors of homes, but out of trepidation, no one answered. The streets were empty. Suddenly, he saw a figure in the distance. He noticed it was a Jew running. The Jew noticed the man from Dubnov as well, and eagerly approached him, calling out, "Fellow Jew, have pity and come along with me." He followed wondering what was needed from him. To his surprise, this Jew informed him that he was seeking a *Minyan* to say *Kaddish*, for a *Yahrzeit* (the anniversary of a death of a close relative), and he was one man short of the required ten.

After the prayers, he took the visitor outside to recite *Kiddush Levana*. How could he go outside during such a moment of danger? The man stated, "Look and see how beautiful the moon is!" The pogroms will continue tomorrow, and is it possible that the moon will not be noticeable?"[105]

The Galitzian Siddur

One of the Jewish soldiers produced a *siddur* (prayer book) from his pocket. It was small, tear-stained, and had quite a story to tell. And this is the remarkable, tragic story he related:

This siddur belonged to an elderly lady from Galitzia, may she rest in peace. The Cossacks (aided by local peasants) would trick the Jews by addressing them in Russian. Since many Jews did not speak that language, they wouldn't understand what the Cossacks wanted. The Cossacks would then drag them to the Russian commandant, and claim that they caught a spy. If the Jews did not understand the conversation, they had no idea they were in mortal danger. The

---

105. Ibid. p. 98

Commandant trusted his underlings and didn't even ask for a shred of evidence. The unfortunate Jews were taken out to a field and shot in cold blood.

One day, while marching from one place to another, we passed such a killing field. We saw a group of bodies, including men, women and children, lying neglected on the ground. There were 32 bodies in the field in various stages of decomposition.

Near the corpse of an elderly man, we saw a woman, obviously his wife, sitting and crying bitterly. She was weak and emaciated. The woman related that three days earlier the Cossacks came into her village. Those who escaped were saved, but those who stayed behind were arrested.

Her husband was abducted while returning home from synagogue, wearing his *tallit* (prayer shawl) and *tefillin*, (phylacteries) and carted off to the commandant. Her two daughters, who tried to escape, were also caught and arrested. She waited all day and night for their return, to no avail. The following day, she gathered her courage and went to the commandant to inquire about them.

The commandant didn't respond, but one of the peasants took pity on her and brought her to this field where she saw the bodies of her husband and two daughters. The poor woman nearly fainted with shock and horror. She remained sitting there weak and listless.

"Please, I beg of you, bury my husband in a Jewish grave," she cried. "Please give him a Jewish burial."

The soldier continued, "We were twelve Jewish soldiers, and we asked our commander for permission to bury the dead. On the spot we dug two deep pits, one for the men, and the other, for the women. Many of the deceased had blood soaked *siddurim* in their pockets. Most of the prayer books were buried, while we kept the ones that could be salvaged. The old woman gave us her husband's *siddur* as a token of gratitude, "May *Hashem* watch over you and protect you in this war."

When the pits were dug the old woman had one final request, "Please dig a separate grave for my husband, because he was a very saintly and holy man." Despite the lateness of the hour and our exhaustion, we heeded her request. We dug a third grave, and placed the remains of the old man. When we covered the grave, the woman took a stick and marked the spot. Then, we placed the other bodies in the mass graves and covered them as well. One of the soldiers said a *Keil Moleh Rachamim* prayer over the bodies, and we stood with our heads bowed, shedding tears.

The burial process took several hours, and it was very late. The old woman was too weak to return to the village, so one of the soldiers brought her there with his wagon. On the way, after traveling about a mile, the poor woman died from exhaustion and grief. Now there was another body to bury, but we had no more strength to dig. We traveled to the city and gave her remains to the first Jew we met. The old woman merited to be buried in the regular *Beit Olam* (cemetery) in the city.

We cherished the *siddur* she had given us, which we dubbed the "Galitzian Siddur."[106]

Russia

The Russian retreat continued and the persecution against the Jews again intensified within Russia and Poland.

As the Russian army was retreating into Lithuania, the Russian authorities published an espionage allegation that was widely publicized in the press. It became a new rallying cry for anti-Semites throughout Lithuania. Though it would be proven false, the damage was done and setting the record straight was virtually impossible.

Kuzhi is a small town of forty families from the Lithuanian border. A German attack gave way to the slander.

The accusation charged that on the night of April 28, the Jews hid Germans in their cellars and at night they attacked the Russian garrison.

On the night of April 28th the Germans attacked a detachment of Russian infantry regiments while resting in the town of Kuzhi. The Jews were accused of concealing German soldiers in their cellars before Russian troops arrived, and at a signal, they set fire to Kuzhi on all sides. The accusation further stated that the Germans leaped out of the cellars, and rushed to the house which the Russian regional

---

106. Eizenberg, *Milchomo Shtoib*, pp. 8–13

commander was occupying. At the same time, two of the battalions supported by cavalry, attacked the Russians and captured the village.[107]

An official investigation by members of the Social Democratic party which included its leader Alexander Kerensky found that the accusation was a farce. Three deputies of the Duma, traveled to Kuzhi and found a total of six Jewish families had resided there – all but one lived in squalid conditions. Their homes were clearly unable to hide any significant numbers of German soldiers. They also discovered that those few Jews had actually left with the permission of the authorities the day before the German invasion on April 27. The Jews of of Kuzhi had spent the night of April 27 in Minstok, another town.[108] However, the tale had already spread, and the denials were to no avail. The libel had become a rallying cry against the Jews. The Kuzhi libel set the stage for one of the most devastating expulsions in Jewish history since the exile of the Jews from Judea in Roman times.

On May 5, 1915[109] – the same day as the Shavuot holiday – over 200,000 Jews in Lithuania and Courland (Latvia) were abruptly forced from their homes into dire circumstances.

While preparing for the upcoming Shavuot holiday, notices appeared calling for the Jews living in areas closer to the warfront to vacate their homes within twenty-four, sometimes forty-eight hours. Most of the notices gave 24 hours, and sometimes even less.

In just a few days, much of Lithuanian Jewry in the area of Kovno, whose legacy goes back hundreds of years, made a hasty exit. They were ordered to move eastward. Even the sick and the infirmed were included in the decree. Those who did not comply faced execution.

With the evening of May 5th approaching, multitudes of Jews headed out into an environment of unknown perils in a desperate search for refuge. Out in the open fields and roads facing numerous dangers, *Kiddush* (prayer over wine sanctifying the holiday) for the holidays was recited and *Minyanim* (quorums) were organized to recite the holiday prayers.

---

107. "The Jews of the Eastern War Zone," p.48
108. Ibid. p. 49
109. According to the Russian calendar the date was May 5, however on the Gregorian calendar the date was May 19.

In Courland, (Latvia) Jews faced a similar fate, although the expulsion was enforced a day or two later.

As the exodus commenced in the town of Keidan, according to an eye-witness, "People bid farewell. They slept on their bundles as cannon fire shook the walls of their homes." Thirty carts filled with men, women, and children on Friday May 8, headed towards the city of Homel. From there they would be forced further East.[110]

A Jewish military physician watched as hundreds of Jews of the town of Keidan quickly gathered their belongings. In shock and despair he asked them why they were being expelled. They responded, "because we are Jews!" With tears in his eyes he replied, "I risk my head for them and they exile my brothers."[111]

The mood in Lithuania defied description.

In Ponevezh, curious members of the local population turned up at the station. "There was real pandemonium in the carriages. Household goods, hurriedly bundled into bags, tablecloths, baskets, trunks – everything was jumbled together. Children lost their parents, who frantically raced around searching for them; the wails of children, the groans of the sick, wailing, shouting. They had brought the people from the almshouse. Blind old men with shaking hands, stricken by paralysis, old women with knapsacks . . . The fatally ill were laid on pitiful rags at the very roadbed." This is how an eyewitness described the expulsions from Ponevezh:[112]

> In areas within the Kovno Governorate, the order was announced on May 2 and 3, and the people were given until the evening of May 5. In the Lithuanian city of Shavli, on the morning of May 2, the district police officer and superintendent announced to the Jews that they were to leave the town within a period of eight hours. Earnest requests led to the deadline being extended to 24 hours. On May 3, the Jewish population left the town. In smaller towns, which had received the order late, on

---

110. Pesach Chittim, (anonymous), Keidan, *Sefer Zikaron*, Hotza'at Irgun Yotzei Keidan B'Yisrael, Tel Aviv, 1977, p. 129

111. Ibid.

112. Simon Dubnov, *Black Book of Russian Jewry*, p. 239

the 3rd, the 4th or even the 5th, the authorities, represented by village police sergeants and superintendents, refused to grant any extensions and mercilessly drove them away.

In small settlements, they didn't stand on ceremony.

> In Veliuona, the police announced: "Yids, get out of the town! Be out within two hours, or else you'll be hanged!" In Rum-kishki, the Jews, already aware of the expulsion in neighboring settlements, awaited their fate. However, there was no village police sergeant, and there was no one to drive them away. On May 5, a guard arrived with a set of documents. The Jews sur-mised that it contained the order for their expulsion. A village police sergeant arrived during the night, and by the morning, the order had been given for the Jews to leave the village. In some places, the police demanded that the Jews be expelled immediately, but agreed to extend the deadline until May 5 for a bribe.[113]

Jewish communities bestowed tremendous kindness upon one an-other. Assistance was offered to refugees arriving at their towns, which included food, lodging, and sometimes employment. The Yekapo organization, the "Jewish Community Relief War Victims" would wait at train stations and other locations to offer aid. There is no telling how much more disastrous the expulsions would have been without the lifesaving work of the Yekapo. Sometimes, the very communities assisting the refugees would soon become refugees themselves, forced out by the same decree.

Some exiles went to Vilna. One rabbi described the reaction of the Vilna community to their arrival, "It was the first day of Shavuot and the Jews of Vilna went to synagogue not knowing that the first train with all those expelled was already arriving at Novo-Vileika . . . Notwithstanding that it was a holy day, meeting places were quickly organized and each Jewish family of Vilna was required to bring something edible . . . In the course of two hours, thousands

---

113. Ibid.

of kilograms of bread, sugar, meat, cheese, eggs, boiled meat and herring were collected."[114]

In Shavli, some men were doing correctional labor a few versts[115] from the town. These Jews knew nothing of the expulsions. When they returned to the town, they could not find their families and did not know where they had gone.[116]

The Ponevezh almshouse had been home to forty-three elderly people. The youngest of them was sixty-seven, the oldest ninety-seven. But those expelled from other places included people over the age of one hundred.[117]

The numbers belie the hardships faced by each individual who suffered and endured. The exiles from Courland asked the administration of Riga if they could leave behind a cripple who had lost both his legs. The administration refused. In Yasvon (Kovno Governorate), Eli Gafenberg's 30-year-old son had been stricken down by paralysis and had been bedridden for the past twelve years. The police did not allow him to be left behind in Yasvon. The bed was placed on a cart, and the sick man completed the long and torturous move. In Vilki, the dying Freida Vilenchuk was put on a cart. Two hours later, she died on the road. Chaim Fishelevich's wife, Pesya, was close to death. He begged the police superintendent, weeping, to permit him to stay. He was driven out of the town with whips. His dying wife was left behind. During the expulsion from Veliuona, as soldiers chased out the community, Freida Dratvin died on the road. She was overcome and fell down. No one could help her as the soldiers would not allow any stopping. Faivel Schwartz, one of the sick people expelled from Kėdainiai, died on the road.[118]

The number of cases are too devastating to list.

One exile reported,

> In Starodub, the Jewish committee had already organized. We initially stayed in the Synagogue, where the local Jews did their

---

114. Pesach Chittin, (Anonymous), Keidan Book, p. 130
115. A Russian measure of length, about .66 mile or 1.1 km
116. Simon Dubnov, *Black Book of Russian Jewry*, p. 240
117. Ibid. p. 239
118. Ibid. p. 241

best to help our situation. They rented us apartments, found us work and enrolled the children in *Cheders* and schools. . . . I particularly remember an extended family by the name of Lushkin, who worked hard to absorb us along with the rest of the community.[119]

The Jewish community set up meal stations *en* route, medical assistance, and sent commissioners with the trains. Inquiries were made about children and relatives who had gone missing. This prevented a catastrophe – mass deaths and wholesale insanity. Then again, there was already hardly a single train that did not contain people who had become mentally deranged from the ordeal.[120]

Some of the exiles were sent directly to districts to the East that had been assigned for settlement. Some were dispersed to the towns and villages of neighboring areas, taking shelter in synagogues, sheds, and sometimes under open skies. Some had passports, and they were able to choose their place of residence. Others, in place of documents, had travel certificates issued in haste by the local authorities.[121]

One after the next, trains went to the east and to the south. One train which took ten days to travel from Pozvol to Unecha was not opened, and no one was let out. At the Unecha station, most of the exiles were in a half-dead state. Sixteen people were sick with scarlet fever, and one person with typhus was removed. All the exiles from the train which arrived in Zolotonosha on May 12 were thrown out onto the railway bed and spent two hours in the pouring rain. The district police officer would not let them into the town, and they were sent back to Kovno.[122]

The following observations describe the very grim plight of Jewish refugees in flight.

A report by Russian author Achevosky stated:

> Hunger, dirt. Lack of air encourages every kind of sickness among them.

---

119. Ibid. Pesach Chittin, (Anonymous), Keidan Book, p. 130
120. Ibid. p. 243
121. Ibid. pp. 241–242
122. Ibid. p. 242

"Have you any invalids?" I asked them. They point out numbers in each carriage.

"Has the doctor seen them?"

"No."'

"What illnesses have they?" Everyone has pain in the stomach. I go near one of these invalids on the floor. The symptoms are dysentery, sickness, and convulsions. "It is obvious he has Cholera!"[123]

In another carriage among the dirty rags a woman is stretched. Her face is covered with a handkerchief.

"Is she ill?" I ask.

"Dead."

"Since when?"

"This morning."

I look at the dead woman. It is four o'clock: the corpse is not removed. Disinfection is not attempted; no one bothers about it. Yesterday the woman – then alright – was attending to her children. She became ill last night.

"Are there any others dead?"

"There are many" is the reply.[124]

In another first-hand account in the Russian Newspaper, *Russkis Slovo*, quoted by the London Jewish Chronicle, Achevosky said:

At the end of the station at Oufa, there are numerous trains filled with fugitives. Close by is the dirty clothing, children playing close to the carriages. Everywhere the same picture. They are crowded into piles, so to speak, old men, children, invalids, exhausted by the long journey [. . .] among the utensils and furniture, most of which is useless, only what was at hand having been collected haphazard. All are in rags: it is a fearful spectacle of black misery. I pass from one carriage to another try[ing] to engage in conversation. No one understands Russian: Most of them are Lithuanians, Ukrainians and Jews.

---

123. *LJC*, December 15, 1915, p. 9
124. *LJC*, Ibid. p. 9

Incomprehensible languages are being spoken. I ask one a question and he gives no answer. Another explains in bad Russian: "He does not understand foreigners." "What language does he speak?" "Only Ukrainian: that carriage is full of refugees from Volhynia." "Where are you going?" "We don't know, they are transporting us we don't know where to." "How long have they been transporting you?" "For a month" says one: "Six weeks," says another. "That doesn't matter" says another. "But why not tell us where they are taking us?" "Someone said it was to Siberia" interrupts one. "And why should we be taken to Siberia? It little matters where they take us so it is nearer to death," says another with resignation. Deeply touched I continue to question these unhappy people. "What have you eaten today?" "Not yet, we are still waiting." They promised to give us some food each day." "And when did you eat last?" "Two days ago."[125]

Back then, all roads in Lithuania led to Vilna, and many of those expelled flowed there. Some managed to move in with relatives in Vilna, and afterwards, when the Germans captured the city, they were able to return home. Many refugees were sent to Novy Shebintziani where the railway split off in different directions so that they could be moved to the interior of Russia and Siberia. The Cossacks hemmed them on all sides and urged them to hurry to undertake the journey they had prepared for them. For the most part, the refugees were divided up on the basis of their cities of origin – former residents of these cities here, former residents of the other cities there. But because of the chaos and commotion, and because of the fear of the Cossacks' whips, the wretched refugees had no time to organize themselves. Their bags were wrested away from them; thousands of families were scattered to the four winds. Fathers were put on trains to Siberia, children to the interior of Russia – and not even to the same cities: one child here, another one there. Hundreds of children were left as orphans of living parents, suddenly bereft of mother and father, brothers and sisters, never to find one another again.[126]

---

125. Quoted from *LJC*, October 15, 1915, p. 9
126. *Ha'ivri*, 5676 (1916), issues 25, 26; Mr. Mordechai Katz *Ha'ivri* 5676 (1916),

A Jewish journalist wrote, "The pen cannot describe the suffering of the refugees on the road. Some three thousand people were stuffed into every train; the cars were full to overflowing. Hungry and thirsty, sick and dying, they traveled for three or four consecutive months before arriving – broken, torn and skeletal – to their destinations. Some, of course, died on the way in terrible agony. The dead would continue to travel in the same cars as the living for days at a time until it was possible to stop and bury them. One can only imagine what it was like to sit near these bodies . . . It is no wonder that some people lost their minds, having seen sights like these."[127]

The condition of the refugees hardly improved once they came to their new locations. The lack of housing forced them to live, for months on end, in cellars, ruins, stables and barns. When lying down to sleep on the shelves that served as beds, they used to say: "One must now crawl into one's grave," because the beds looked like burial niches and graves.[128]

By the 5th of May, 1915, on Shavuot, at midnight, there were no Jews remaining at the border of the entire area that was set to be empty of Jews by order of the Czarist "High Command." Many banished Lithuanian Jews were not able to travel by wagon. They dragged themselves on foot until beaten, hungry and exhausted they reached a train station, or a larger Jewish center in the Jewish pale of settlement such as Vilna. Announcements of Jewish refugees searching for lost children and relatives were not published in the Russian newspapers. The censor did not want the sad, true situation of the exiled Jews to be publicized, because this would compromise the government and the military staff in the eyes of the world at large.[129]

There were Russian writers and politicians who spoke out against the persecution.

Even at the beginning of the war, at its December 19, 1914 session, the Municipal Council of Smolensk passed a resolution petitioning

---

quoted from Graubart, *Sefer Zikaron*, p. 265

127. Ibid.

128. Ibid.

129. American Jewish Committee Yearbook, Jewish Publication Society America, Philadelphia, PA, 1915–1916

the government to "abolish all measures which restrict the rights of Russian subjects of the Jewish faith."[130]

One manifesto issued early in the war by leading Russian publicists and writers protesting anti-Semitism stated, "The sorely-tried Jewish nation which has given to the world such precious contributions in the domain of religion, of philosophy, of poetry; which has always shared the travails and trials of Russian life . . . is now again subject to unjust accusations and persecutions."[131]

Acknowledging the oppression of Jews, Social Democrat Party Duma member, Nikolai Tchkiedze – a non-Jew – protested.

> In the name of what humanity is it forbidden to hand food to starving Jewish refugees cooped up in freight trains? In the name of what brotherhood is one part of the army aroused against the Jewish soldiers who are in the trenches side by side with our own soldiers? We accuse the Germans of breaking the laws of warfare, of using poison gas and mutilating prisoners. But, gentlemen, in the name of what laws of humanity are orders issued to the Russian army to drive peaceful Jews ahead of the troops and expose them to fire?[132]

Yet another show of opposition occurred at a military industrial committee meeting in May, 1915, one speaker, Professor E.L. Zubashov, calls for the abolition of all restrictive measures against the Jews. He was met with thunderous applause.[133]

Post Shavuot

The expulsion decree of May 1915 did not last. Soon after, commander in chief of the Russian armies, Nikolai Nikolayevich, informed the military authorities that mass expulsions of Jews were no

---

130. Ibid. p. 77
131. Ibid. p. 82
132. On Aug. 3, 1915, *Jews in the Eastern War Zone*, American Jewish Committee, pp. 72–73
133. Ibid. p. 80

longer desired since the economy was damaged as a result.[134] It is also very conceivable that international pressure, especially from the United States whose participation in the war effort was desperately sought by the allies, impacted that change. Nikolayevich proposed that Jews should be expelled only from one specific place at a time, in "exceptional cases."[135]

The news of the suspension and cancellation of the expulsion unleased a wave of joy throughout the areas among the exiles. But this joy was limited. The Jews would not agree to the demand that they sign the verdict on their alleged disloyalty and confirm it by dispatching hostages. The vast majority of exiles rejected this cruel and humiliating proposal and refused to voluntarily furnish hostages.[136]

Young Jews, who had just been expelled on the eve of conscriptions, were ordered to return immediately to serve. Just before the conscriptions, notices were posted in the Kovno Governorate: "It is announced by the Kovno Governor that with the permission of the commander of the tenth army that Jews of the 1916 conscription are permitted to report to the location of the military units in areas cleansed from Jews for the duration of the conscription until being sent off to join the troops."[137]

Expulsions of Jews by the high command did continue for the next few months.

In July, 1915, the Germans launched an attack in the Baltic Region to the North and also turned towards the Kovno and Vilna Governorates of Lithuania. Military action moved eastwards from the line of the May expulsions. At the end of July, after Warsaw had been taken, the enemy intensified its activities in the Vilna-Kovno region in Lithuania. On August 5, evacuations began from Vilna, although the town remained in Russian hands until early September. Kovno, a Jewish center, fell on August 7. In early September, the German

---

134. The expulsions did continue in Galitzia.
135. Simon Dubnov, *Black Book of Russian Jewry*, p. 246
136. Ibid. p. 247
137. The American Jewish Chronicle, November 11, 1916, p. 448

advance guard entered the Minsk Governorate in Belorussia. Areas often changed hands, sometimes several times. The retreat of Russian troops was accompanied all along the line by anti-Jewish pogroms, and often by the wholesale expulsion of the Jewish population, undertaken for the most part on the orders of a staging officer, and sometimes even at the discretion of the soldiers, without any orders whatsoever from above.

With the mass expulsions came the end of the Pale Settlement, which had forcibly confined Russian Jewry to restricted boundaries since the rule of Czarina Catherine the Great, at the end of the 18th century. The Eastern border needed to be opened to Jews to allow for the flight of refugees. Despite the growing opposition within segments of Russia to the persecution of Russian Jewry, it was not the voices in protest but necessity that ended the Pale Settlement.

Expulsions Soon Resumed and Pogroms Continue

As the Germans continued their push, expulsions and pogroms continued. At the start of September, the Jews were expelled from a number of settlements in the vicinity of Luninets, a small city in southern Belarussia. A pogrom took place in Luninets itself. In Vulka and Luncheke, also in Belarus, a twelve-hour period was provided for their departure; in Khmelnik, Dubkovichi and Bogdanovka, they were given two hours. The expulsions were accompanied by the destruction of their property.[138]

Could pogroms have been prevented? One menacing shout from an officer could have been sufficient for the instigators to disperse, or even the intervention by non-officers coming to the rescue.

There were those who prevented violence. Without commanders who protected Jewish communities, the destruction would have been even more severe. In Friedrichstadt, the honest, universally-loved head of the district refused to allow violence. In Vilna, the army commander, General Rodkevich, brought calm demanding that the population not allow unrest, and threatened severe punishment for

---

138. Russian Jewry: Dubnov, *Black Book of Russian Jewry*, pp. 288–289

violators. In Vileyka, the commander ordered that the Jews not be touched. But such cases were not the norm.[139]

Jewish Soldiers Coming to Their Aid

There were many instances of Jewish soldiers coming to the aid of fellow Jews. Jewish soldiers in some situations regularly visited Jewish families to ensure their welfare. In some places, Jewish soldiers shared their last crusts of bread with local Jews suffering from hunger. During a pogrom in Sokol, Jewish soldiers together with Cossacks plundered food items from stores and then they quietly returned them to their owners.[140] It the small town of Lukhatov, Shalom Ansky reported of a Jewish soldier named Yisroel Vaysbard, who provided funds and food to its Jewish community for half a year. Stories of Vaysbard in that town were legendary.[141]

During a Cossack pogrom, a fight broke out between the Cossacks and the Jewish soldiers, which continued onto the street. Two Jewish soldiers were killed and many injured. Cossacks were also badly injured. The commander ordered that all the participants in the fight be arrested and sent to the front.[142] Other such incidents occurred.

Despite the strict ban on fraternizing, soldiers secretly visited local Jews, gave them advice on how to cope and helped them in any way they could. In many places, a Jewish soldier virtually became part of a family and there were cases of soldiers who courted real danger on behalf of fellow Jews. There were incidents when Cossacks were abusing women, and Jewish troops who happened to be nearby fired at the Cossacks killing many of them."[143]

The sufferings of Jewish women during this period deserve a special place in the martydom of Russian Jewry. There was scarcely a single pogrom that was not accompanied by cases of violence against women. In a number of pogroms (Smarhon, Glubokoye, Vidzy,

---

139. Ibid. p. 289
140. Shalom Ansky, *Churban HaYehudim*, p. 94
141. Ibid. p. 95
142. Dubnov, *Black Book of Russian Jewry*, p. 283
143. Ansky p. 80

Lemeshevichi and others), the violence took on mass proportions. There were some pogroms where there was not one woman who was not violated.

The appearance in the town of Cossack detachments, which did not spare either young girls or old women, caused terrible panic amongst Jewish women. Neither did those perpetrating the violence take mercy on the wives of soldiers.[144]

Jews Singled Out

The Jews were specifically maligned, targeted, and persecuted on account of their identity as Jews.

Many civilians of different nationalities also faced expulsions and suffered. Poles of German origins, Russian Germans, as well as Galitzians, Ukrainians, and Serbs suffered from the Russian scorched-earth policy, which left nothing of value for the enemy. Farms were destroyed by retreating Russian forces to leave nothing for the Germans. The numbers of refugees throughout these regions was staggering. However such abuse was generally tactical. Jews received severe treatment out of the hatred harbored against them by the perpetrators. They faced accusations of treason, suffered violence, abuse, and atrocities unlike any other ethnic groups in the Eastern European war zones.

The excerpts in the next chapter have been adapted from the book, *Milchomoh Shtoib*, (War Dust) by Shimon Zev Eizenberg, from Uzabon, Lithuania, who wrote of the personal experiences of a refugee at the time of the Shavuot expulsion from the Kovno region of Lithuania on the eve of the Shavuot holiday in 1915. Initially, the family had fled the approaching German advance and unknowingly found themselves in the middle of the mass expulsion, wandering from one town and city to another, not knowing what the next day would bring.

---

144. Ibid. p. 292

Chapter 3

How Long is the Night?

The following stories and events took place when Lithuania was under Russian control, until it was conquered by the Germans in the spring of 1915.

April 22, 1915

The homeless Jews who entered our little shtetl pleaded for bread and water, and then continued running to safety. They were literally starving, desperate for food. An old man with a heavy load on his back passed me and said, "Reb Yid, why are you standing here? Why aren't you running away?"

"Where should I run to?" I replied. "Should I leave my home empty, for it to be plundered? What about my poor family?"

"If you don't run away now," the old man threatened, "the gunners will catch up to you, and you won't live to see tomorrow."

The Germans soon conquered our village. They consorted with the Christian girls and took everything they saw. Thousands of German soldiers, wielding cannons, passed in the late afternoon. They rampaged through our village like hungry lions taking the wounded Russian soldiers as prisoners.

Suddenly, in the middle of the night a contingent of soldiers banged on our door and burst inside, demanding food. They told us to leave the door open so that they can find shelter. They then laid down on our beds, and we were forced to remain awake, shivering in fear. "Wake us up at 3:00 a.m.," they demanded, "and not a moment later."

The commanding officer was asleep on my sofa, and I remained awake, anxiously waiting for 3:00 a.m. The minutes passed slowly, but eventually wake-up time arrived. I unsuccessfully tried to awaken the soldier from his deep slumber. So I pulled his feet until at last, with great difficulty, he opened his eyes.

With a loud noise and commotion he awakened the other soldiers. They were exhausted and weary, with no strength, thoroughly sick of battle. "When will this bloody war end?" they asked each other.

The officers then rampaged through our home, looking for valuables. One soldier took a candle and went down to the cellar, going through each room. One room was locked because it belonged to another family. He broke open the lock and helped himself to its contents.[145]

Slander

One day I saw the German soldiers running through our village in a frenzy. What happened?

"Military exercises," they said tersely. We didn't believe them. In the end, we realized that the Russians had arrived. They were preparing a takeover, to drive out the Germans. The tide for the mean time had turned in favor of the Russian army.[146]

Suddenly the Lithuanian peasants, who had tried to curry favor with the Germans, wanted to ingratiate themselves to the Russians. They began spreading rumors that the Jews had been spying for the Germans. The Russians readily accepted these lies and turned against the Jews. An old man, on his way to synagogue approached me and asked, "What do we do now? We are lost." He related that a Russian soldier saw him and said, "Go away, or I will shoot you like a dog, Jew. You German spy."

145.

146. Chapter one in *Milchomoh Shtoib, Zichronos Fun a Yiddishe Palit*, (Memoirs of a Jewish Refugee 1915–1917) Klerksdorf Publisher, 1922, pp. 1–8

I warned the old man to stay home and not walk in the street if he values his life.

On the way back to our base, we passed more mud fields, filled with bodies of Jews wearing *talliit kotons*. It was a terrible sight. Yet we had no more time or energy to bury them. The other cities we passed were completely empty and "*Judenrein*," or cleared of Jews. Their homes were pillaged and vandalized by the Russians.

Author Shimon Zev Eizenberg: when I heard of the terrible suffering the Jews in other areas had experienced, I felt that we were the fortunate ones.

Kuz, circa Expulsion of Shavuot 1915

I, Shimon Zev Eisenberg, live in Abazon. One day, I notice several horses, some hitched to wagons, wandering around in fear. They seem to have escaped from the nearby village of Kuz. I heard that the Russians had recently annexed the area while the Germans went into hiding.

One night at 11:00 p.m. the Germans burst out of the barn stalls. There were no Russian soldiers around, as they had all gone to sleep. The Germans set the house where the governor lived, on fire, and shot him in his sleep. The Russians, sleepy and confused, rushed out into the street and began shooting each other.

The Germans were on a rampage. They shot up the railroad tracks, burned down houses, and shot anyone they encountered. The terrified Jews went into hiding. Some hid in the trenches along with the Russians soldiers. They were just as afraid, even more so than the Russians.

We were not aware of this in Abazon. Suddenly, the town square was filled with frightened men, on horseback or riding on wagons, who escaped from Kuz. They related the horrors that had occurred. They falsely blamed the Jews for the trouble and for hiding the Germans in their homes providing them with food. They also told them where the Russian commanders were hiding.

An old woman came into town, riding her horse, attached to a wagon. The frightened woman asked, "Did you see my brother? He is the priest of Kuz."

"Your brother?" one of the men from Kuz said. "You mean our local priest? He is dead; the Germans killed him." The old woman began to weep and wail over her brother, cursing the Jews she accused of being responsible for his death.

The Jews of Abazon were terrified. They sensed a pogrom was coming. And indeed, within moments, the local peasants began to call for a pogrom.

The blacksmith, the tailor, the water-carrier, and soon the local peasants were whipped into a frenzy. They began to rouse their neighbors, telling them about all the terrible crimes of the Jews. "They gave up the Governor's location, and the Germans shot him. They even enabled the priest to be killed by the enemy. It is our job to avenge his blood."

We tried to explain to our neighbors that they were playing a vicious game, "You want to kill the Jews and plunder their property, so you are slandering them, pouring oil on the fire. "

"Now that the Russians are in power, you slander us and say we are German spies! We have suffered under German rule just like you have, and sometimes even more. Our houses were burned, our children killed. How dare you suspect us!"

Our heartfelt words fell on deaf ears. No one wanted to listen to the truth. Instead, the cries of "Death to the Jews!" only grew stronger. "We will kill you, we will slit your throats and shoot you!" they shouted.

We began to fear that death was imminent. Who would protect us? Where would we hide?

And then, suddenly, several bombers swooped down low and began to shoot from the skies. The terrified peasants fled for their lives, and the pogrom was averted . . . for the moment. The peasants were too busy hiding to worry about the Jews. Yet, we knew this was only a temporary reprieve. They would be back.

Several hours passed. The bombers had gone. Suddenly, the priest of Kuz appeared who was supposedly killed by the

Germans after the Jews supposedly betrayed him. He was very much alive, and had not been caught.

"You are alive!" his sister excitedly yelled out. "Praise G-d!" The other gentiles began to sing and dance and the Jews breathed a heavy sigh of relief. The danger was over. Their lives had been spared at the last moment, by a miracle.

Now the shtetl became quiet again, but not for long.[147]

Flight Into Mass Expulsion, Events of Shavuot 1915

The peasants would often pass the time by telling the Russian soldiers tall tales about the Jews. They would say that the Jews are sending gold to Germany to help with the war effort. They would also whisper that the Jews have secret telephones hidden in their beards, and are informing on the Russians, telling the Germans where they are hiding.

During that time, a Jew's blood was cheap. Everyone wanted to "get" the Jew and finish him off: Germans, Russians and Lithuanians all hated the Jew. We wandered alone on the slaughtering grounds of Poland and Lithuania.

Whenever the Germans would attack we would try to escape to the next village, always one step ahead of the enemy. Yet danger awaited us everywhere.

One day, when the Germans entered our city, we tried to escape. We grabbed a few possessions and began to travel to the neighboring village. The journey was dangerous and brutal. All along the paths, we saw household items abandoned: items like pillows, clothes, and even sewing machines. No one looked at them or needed them anymore. Our eyes were only focused skyward, trying to escape the constant aerial bombings.

We passed deep ditches, where we saw overturned wagons and dead horses. The Russian soldiers would strip the horses of their saddles and remove the wheels from the wagons.

As our journey progressed the sights we saw were more horrific. There were bodies in the ditches and lying on the ground,

---

147. Eizenberg, *Milchomo Shtoib*, Chapter 4, from page 23

along with severed limbs. Many of the dead were recognizable, as our own friends and neighbors.

Along the way I met a neighbor who also left my village. "What kind of Jew are you?" he yelled at me in distress, "How can you abandon the shul and the Torah Scrolls? The enemy went into our shul and plundered it. They took the prayer shawls to polish their saddles, and then placed them under the saddle like a lining."

I began to cry and said, "You are right. But what can I do? I was barely able to escape with my small children. How can I risk my life for the synagogue?" We cried together, and then my friend said, "Now is not the time for crying. Our lives are still in danger." So we continued on our journey.[148]

Erev Shavuot, May, 1915

The author continues to relate his saga:

My family and I were traveling in a rented wagon, owned by a gentile driver, Yurgis. We continued traveling through the countryside, which was in a state of chaos. The Germans and Russians were at each other's throats.

We had paid Yurgis generously for his services. Yet when we arrived at the outskirts of the city of Mishkortz, he became very anxious. "I am afraid of the soldiers who are roaming the streets, searching for Jews," our driver confessed.

By that time, it was already dark, and we were hiding in the wagon. Yurgis sat in the driver's seat, guiding the horses. Suddenly he was accosted by a band of soldiers. "Who goes there?" they demanded.

"I am a Christian, and I come from a village near Kuz," he replied confidently.

"Who are you taking with you?" they inquired.

"There was a fire in my village, and I barely escaped with my

---

148. Eizenberg, *Milchomo Shtoib*, Chapter 6, from page 40

family," said Yurgis. "I am heading to my brother's house, where we hope to find shelter."

"Do you have any Jews with you?" they continued. "They should be shot like dogs! They sold us to the Germans!"

I heard the exchange and shuddered.

"Jews?" the driver asked, "There are no accursed Jews in our village!" he said without hesitation. "We got rid of them a long time ago. They give us heartache, and are our enemies. Besides, they hid Germans in their cellars and gave them their gold."

"If we find a Jew," said the soldiers with venom, "We will cut him up into pieces!"

We were trembling in fear. No one dared utter a word. I was almost expecting them to examine the wagon and find us hiding. But it appeared that Yurgis wanted to protect us. He gave them a cigarette, uttered a few more choice curses about the Jews, and they went on their way. "So, what do you say about the job I did?" he joked. "If they would have found you, your lives would not have been worth a kopeck." Needless to say, we thanked him heartily for saving our lives.

We continued riding through the night, exhausted and disheveled. All throughout our journey we heard shooting, and grenades exploding, literally over our heads. The entire countryside was a war zone.

In the morning, as we passed the outskirts of other villages, we saw a large number of wagons, filled to the brim with people and furnishings. Many people were wandering by foot. I quickly identified them as fellow Jews. Tragically, they had been expelled from their homes and were on the run.

"Who are you?" I asked the refugees. "Where are you from?"

"We are from Shavel, [in Lithuania,]" they replied with a sigh. "Shavel is now free of Jews. All of us, (over 15,000 Jews) were expelled from the city in the past 24 hours."

I realized that my own family's plight was not so bad. There were refugees who were hungry, wearing rags, without basic supplies.

"Mama, I'm hungry," I heard a small child cry out from a wagon.

"Soon, my child," the mother tried to calm her son, "Soon, when we will get to the village."

"Mama, when will we go home?" asked a little girl.

"Oy, we don't have a home anymore," sighed the poor woman. I noticed that she was alone with her children, and wondered about the whereabouts of her husband.

"Mama, where is Tatteh?" the first child asked. Another sigh, "My child, Tatteh is very far away, and will not come back for a long time. He was sent to the front."

My heart ached for this poor woman, whose husband was very likely serving as cannon fodder on the front lines, in the trenches.

"Mama, I'm so hungry," another child whined. I felt sorry for the poor woman, who did not have a crust of bread with her. I reached into our own sack and gave her some of my family's supplies. The woman thanked me tearfully, and explained that they had left in such a hurry they had no time to pack provisions.

"My husband was wounded, and he is in a hospital in Cracow," she told us.

Her neighbors had advised her not to go join him, as he would be unable to help her. Instead, she was trying to find a new home for herself and her children. In Shavel, she had earned a decent living as a seamstress. But now she had nothing, no provisions and no home.

We continued riding until we arrived at the outskirts of Ligam, another small shtetl. We were eager to settle somewhere, and remain in one place during the holiday of Shavuot.

By then it was 4:00 a.m., on the morning before Shavuot. Though it was still pitch black outside, the homes were lit up as if it were daylight. This was very strange; normally, in most villages, the houses were dark until the morning! What was going on? Perhaps there was an influx of Jews from Shavel, which had been emptied. In my wildest dreams I could not have imagined the reality.

When we arrived in the center of the village, I stopped at the local shul. To my surprise, I heard screaming and crying coming from within. I was certain a calamity must have occurred.

"What is going on?" I asked, coming inside. "I am a wanderer from a distant city, and am looking for a place to stay for Shavuot. I am willing to pay," I clarified. "My family is very exhausted."

My words were met with incredulous stares. "Are you crazy? You want to stay here? Don't you know what is going on? We have to leave our homes by tomorrow. On the 18th of May, Ligam has to be *Judenrein*."

I was shocked to hear these words. Now I understood the chaos, the screaming, why all the homes were well lit. So Ligam was to be emptied of its Jews, just like all the other towns in Lita. [Lithuania] What have we done to deserve this?

I left the shul to rejoin my family. In the meantime, Yurgis, the wagon driver, had disappeared. But I couldn't worry about that now. We were looking for a place to rest our weary bones, for some warm water to drink.

But there was nowhere to go. The village was engulfed in chaos. Everywhere, people were trying to rent wagons, to place their household goods and furnishings inside. Men, women and children were everywhere, crying and moaning, packing up their belongings. Old men had gone to shul to pick up their *tefillin* and bid goodbye to the House of Prayer.

It was terrible to see their pain and anguish. Yet I didn't have the energy to worry about them; I was too busy worrying about my own family.

Where was our driver? What had he done with our wagon and all our possessions? I desperately ran around the village trying to find him. Finally, towards dawn, he showed up. I reprimanded him, "Where have you been. We were searching for you?"

Yurgis didn't look particularly distressed as he said. "I can't help you anymore. Take your things off my wagon, because I have been hired by another family."

"What? You can't do this to us!" I protested. "We hired you to take us, and we're paying you for your services!"

"The other family offered me more money," he replied. He began to remove our possessions from the wagon.

I stood there, shocked and unable to say a word, but I realized that I had better act before it was too late. "Wait. Don't take our things off!" I pleaded. "How much is the other family giving you?"

Yurgis named a large sum, far more than what I had promised him. Having no choice, I agreed to pay the same price. I breathed a sigh of relief when he agreed. We quickly climbed back into the wagon and left the town.

I sat outside, next to Yurgis, while my family was huddled inside. Despite the fact that it was spring, the weather was chilly, and I shivered in my thin overcoat. We traveled all the way to Pokroy, the next village, where I hoped to finally stop for *Yom Tov*. We wanted to refresh ourselves, have a bite to eat, and cook a hen for the holiday.[149]

By now, the new day had dawned, bringing with it more horrors. The streets were clogged with refugees, some going with the wagon, others by foot. There was lots of crying and moaning, as everyone bewailed their destruction. It seemed surreal, like *"churban Yerushalayim."* [The destruction of the Jerusalem Temple]

We found entire families walking along the road, dragging their heavy sacks. There were mothers with small children who were crying from exhaustion and hunger. I noticed an elderly man leading a goat, which was tied with a string to his belt. On his shoulder he balanced a sack with his possessions. A little boy of about eight, possibly his grandson, walked next to him, also carrying a heavy bundle.

I saw a father surrounded with six small children, each staggering under the load of their heavy bundles. They had been forced to leave their villages and homes, and were dragging their most valuable possessions. Their bags were very heavy, and they kept on stopping to rest, or change their bundles from one hand to another.

I saw an old woman dragging a heavy chair. Every few steps she stopped to rest, and sat down on the chair. She begged us

149. Eizenberg, *Milchomo Shtoib*, Chapter 8, from page 54

75

to make space for her on the wagon, because she was so weak and exhausted. "I can't go on much longer," the old woman said, "or I will die of exhaustion."

I wanted to help her, and even our driver felt sorry for her, but what could we do? There was not a drop of room on our wagon. We were forced to leave her behind.

The procession continued, slowly, trudging along the road. We surveyed the tragic scene of the wandering Jews, alone and bereft. No one knew where they were headed. It was only a few hours before *Yom Tov*, and the atmosphere was beyond belief. I caught a glimpse of a pale, obviously sick young man, who was caring for a few small children. They all looked exhausted.

Along the way we heard an old man sigh. "How can I help you?" I asked. "Do you need anything?" "I am praying for G-d to take my soul," the old man said. "It will be much better for me in the Next World."

Soon we arrived in the middle of a forest. There appeared to be hundreds of people there, gathering twigs to make a fire.

And then, in the forest, we saw a tragic sight. A young woman was sitting under a tree, surrounded by two small children. In her arms she held a small child, who appeared to be asleep. Something about the woman's pitiful expression made me stop.

"Do you need help?" I asked. "Where is your husband?"

The woman began to cry. "I am from Shavel," she said. "They took him away to the front, and I am alone with the children. My little Chaim is very sick with a lung infection. I have been carrying him in my arms all this time. Now I fear he is no longer alive."

I glanced at the child in her arms, and realized that he was no longer breathing. Indeed, it seemed as if his soul had left his body. When we confirmed his death, the children began to cry and scream. The poor mother wrapped her child's body in a cloth and put it under the tree. Then she began to weep and wail in her agony. "Oy, my Chaim, my Chaim!"

A gentile passed with a wagon. Hearing the commotion, he stopped. "Do you want me to take your child's body to the city?" he asked. The woman agreed. At least she would not have to trek through the forest with her dead child in her arms. We wrapped the child in a sack and put it on the wagon, tying the sack so that it should not slip out. Then the poor woman continued walking with her two surviving children.

We continued on our way and saw another Jew praying, crying his heart out to Hashem. "Your prayers are going straight to Heaven," I informed him.

"If Hashem won't listen to us now, when will He listen?" he replied. "Are we such a bad nation? Who isn't praying with a broken heart?"

I listened as this man poured out his tale of woe. He had three sons, but all were drafted into the army. He had no idea how they were, or if they were still alive. He had not received a letter from them in some time as he was driven out of his home. His wife died recently of a broken heart.

"I envy my wife," he said to me in all seriousness. "At least she is finally at peace, while I am all alone."

As we left the forest, I saw a most unusual couple: a husband with his blind wife, each of them carrying a heavy package. The woman was complaining, "I have no strength to travel anymore. How much farther do we have to go?"

"I don't know," replied the man tersely. Seeing that he had observers, he burst into an angry tirade.

"May Czar Nikolai be cursed for ordering us out of our homes! May the Russians become as blind as my wife! Other people can go where they want, and I have to drag this heavy package through the woods!"

"Perhaps we can hire a wagon?" the woman asked timidly.

He burst into another round of angry criticism. "You keep on complaining! Don't be such a madam. How do you expect me to get a wagon? You are always asking for something or another! This is wartime and I have no way to get a wagon. From where should I get the money?"

He paused for breath and continued, "Do you think this is bad? The true *tzoros*, [pain and suffering] are still going to come. Wait and see."

"Why are you so angry?" the poor woman asked. "Will it please you if I die?"

"You won't die, Shprintza" said her husband. "You will live and live, and suffer."

I couldn't stand his attitude, and decided to give him a piece of my mind. "Reb Yid, why are you so angry at your wife? She is blind, and sick, and has no strength. Be grateful that she is carrying a heavy package!"

"Do you know what I suffer from her at home?" he asked me angrily.

"Why do you make her suffer more?" I retorted, but I saw it was useless to argue. We left this unhappy couple and continued to the shtetl of Pokroy.[150]

By now it was late afternoon on Erev Shavuot. The streets were congested, thronged with thousands of horses and carriages, as well as travelers trekking by foot. We were exhausted beyond words, desperate to find a place to rest. But where would we stop? My wife remembered that she had an elderly uncle in Pokroy. We arrived at his home and I knocked on the door.

"Who is there, and what do you want?" he asked.

"I am your nephew, and I am looking for a place to rest," I replied.

"I have no room," he said, gesturing to all the refugees crammed into his home. Then he slammed the door.

I asked my wife to try her luck. Perhaps her uncle would take pity on her. She knocked on the door and her uncle recognized her immediately.

"How are you?" he asked. "What are you doing here?"

"We ran away from the shooting and grenades," my wife said. "Please, can we shelter in your home?"

"What home? I have no home," her uncle replied. "We have to leave the city by this evening, at six o'clock."

"I have no strength to continue," my wife said. "Can we please come inside, at least for a while to rest?"

Her uncle had pity on us and allowed us to squeeze into

---

150. Eizenberg, *Milchomo Shtoib*, Chapter 9, from page 63

their tiny home, which was already full of people. We cooked some water, drank tea, and tried to cook our hen. The hours passed, but our uncle made no move to pack his possessions. It was nearly *Yom Tov*, and soon the deadline to leave the city would arrive. His wife, our aunt, was baking dairy foods for the holiday, as if everything was the same.

"Uncle, why don't you pack up?" I finally asked him. He looked at me, his face weary.

"Where will we go? And for how long?"

"We don't know, Uncle. Everywhere, Jews are being driven out of their homes. Perhaps it will take months until we can return, or perhaps never. In any case, we can help you pack."

"How can they tell us to leave?" he asked, angry and hurt. "This is my parents' home. We have lived here for generations."

What could we tell him? We described the devastation we had witnessed on the streets.[151]

As the afternoon turned into evening, the streets of Pokroy were filled with great misery. Men, women and children hurried out of the shtetl clutching their tattered possessions. It was the same sorry sight all over again. I heard that the Jewish doctors of Pokroy were given permission to stay behind, but they refused to abandon their brothers, and gallantly joined them in their wandering.

It was nearly 6:00 and we had to leave. As we walked out into the street, we could hear a Jewish shopkeeper tell his gentile neighbor, "I am leaving, and I want you to take care of my shop until I return. Please have mercy on me and keep it for me. I worked so hard to build a thriving business, and I don't want to lose it." I felt sorry for the man, and knew that it was useless, his shop was finished. The gentiles were gleefully awaiting the moment that they would plunder all the goods in the shops.[152]

It was *Ne'ila* time, the final deadline.

At 6:00 p.m. the church bells began to ring, their chimes

---

151. Eizenberg, *Milchomo Shtoib*, Chapter 10, from page 71
152. Eizenberg, *Milchomo Shtoib*, Chapter 11, from page 78

mournful. They seemed to be crying together with us. Soon the police were swarming all over the village driving out the Jews. There was terrible screaming and chaos as the last stragglers were thrown out of their homes. Sadly, I was already accustomed to the terrible sight.

We continued traveling on the wagon as *Yom Tov* arrived. I soon heard a Rabbi, sitting on a wagon with his family, making *kiddush* on two challahs. He said the bracha of *Atoh Bochartonu*, You have chosen us, with tears in his eyes. Even the angels cried along.

"Why are you crying?" I asked him. "It's *Yom Tov*, after all."

"My dear friend, I know I shouldn't cry," he replied. "I don't want to ruin the holiday, but my heart is broken. I am embarrassed of the gentiles, who are saying that Jewish blood is free for all. We are worse than the dogs."

And then he began to cry, "Hashem, what have you done to Your nation on the beautiful night of Shavuot, the giving of the Torah? Could You not have chosen another night? All these years we have celebrated our relationship with You, and now this?" He began to argue with G-d. His devotion and caring for his fellow Jews caused him to speak thus.

It has been many years since that night, yet the Rabbi's *kiddush* and heartbreak are seared into my memory.

It was late at night by the time we arrived in Yaneskel, and the Jews had already been driven out. We were allowed to stay in the empty shul, whose windows were boarded but for just a short while. A gentile, who had the key to the shul and the Rav's house, permitted us to enter.

The Rabbi's house was filled with the scent of challahs the Rebbetzin had baked before they were driven away. We sat down and enjoyed our meager meal. We drank tea and rested our bones. The gentile waited impatiently for us to leave. We gave him some of our rolls, in order to persuade him to let us stay a bit. Our uncle and aunt, who had come with us, were very depressed. Our aunt refused to eat anything.

We went back onto the wagon, our hearts a bit lighter. "Nu," I said to my wife. "We are among Jews, and will be okay. A bit of challah, some warm tea, and we feel much better. See, our G-d is not asleep!"

Then I marveled at how we had become homeless, wandering Jews, just concerned about our food and drink, not worrying about the future.

The night was chilly, and the children slept fretfully. I leaned on a package and tried to doze off, yet the church bells of Pokroy still reverberated in my brain. We continued riding to Pasval. Suddenly, the buggy bumped into a rock and the entire wagon shook. We all woke up, startled. All around us we heard small children crying with exhaustion. It was surreal.

The situation of the elderly and sick was pitiful. Many were near death. We saw a sick young mother in a wagon. Her husband followed by foot exclaimed with worry, "I hope she will survive the journey." She had just given birth to a child and was very weak. The doctors did not allow her to leave her bed, yet they were driven out of the village by the ruthless peasants.

"How long is this night," the poor young man cried. "Oy, when will it be morning?"

As we passed the peasants, we saw them sitting in their homes, relaxed, eager to see us leave. No one was bothering them or throwing them out. Only we were homeless, during that long, endless night. Everyone waited eagerly for the interminable night to end.[153]

We finally arrived in Pasval at 5:00 in the morning. Though it was in May, it was a frigid morning, and we were shivering with cold. Wherever I looked I saw wagons filled with the sick and dying, the elderly and small children, who were groaning from cold and hunger.

Pasval itself was empty of Jews, as they, too, had been thrown out of their homes before Shavuot.

I knew I needed some warm drinks for my frightened, exhausted children. They could not be found as the gentiles had taken over the Jewish homes. We followed some of the refugees to the synagogue in Pasval, which was wide open. The Torah

---

153. Eizenberg, *Milchomo Shtoib*, Chapter 12, from page 85

scrolls were still in the *Aron Kodesh*. Inside, the main sanctuary looked like a hospital – the sick were lying on the ground, the wet children were being changed, and people were preparing food. Some had even bought food from the gentiles; they sold a bucket of water for the tidy sum of ten kopeks. It was Shavuot, after all, and they wanted to prepare their *Yom Tov* meal. Others were sleeping, people were milling about – the scene was utter chaos. We only had until 11:00 to remain there, before we would also be driven out.

On the side, a deathly ill woman was attended by a doctor. Soon she showed signs of improvement, and her children rejoiced. Their mother would live to take care of them!

As I observed the commotion, I noticed the Rabbi of Shavel, Rabbi Meir Atlas, who had joined the refugees in the synagogue. It was Shavuot, and he wanted to pray with a *minyan*. After the initial commotion subsided, an elderly man approached the *bimah* and began to recite the words, *Shochein Ad* [He who dwells above, his Name is holy]. Many of those assembled joined the *minyan*. We were homeless refugees, but we still needed to pray.

What a scene in that synagogue! The crying of the children, groaning of the elderly, and the voices of the men immersed in prayer mingled with the squawking of the hens that were roaming around! The chickens kept on disturbing the prayers, until someone put his hand on their beaks to quiet them down.

Soon *Shacharit* [morning prayers] was over, and it was time to say *Hallel*. What *Hallel?* Who could say *Hallel* in such a time.

"No, we don't have to say *Hallel*," the men protested. "It's not Shavuos today. It's actually Tisha B'av, the day of the destruction of the third *Beis Hamikdash*. We should say *Kinos*, not *Hallel*. How can we thank G-d on such a day, when we were driven out of our homes like dogs? Even G-d wouldn't want our *Hallel* today."

We all stood there weeping, our hearts beating with emotion. Everyone felt the poignant emotions of this sad *Yom Tov*, the day the Torah was given, when we were homeless, penniless, sick and hungry. The tension at those moments could be cut with a knife.

The holy Rabbi Meir Atlas stood there, with his head bent, sharing our sorrows.[154] Rabbi Meir then banged on the *bimah*, looked at our pale faces, and said, in a ringing voice, "Children, it will pass. Everything will pass. Thousands of years of pain and suffering have already passed. This is the will of Hashem. And now, children, let us say *Hallel*."

We all began to weep, our bitter tears mingling as one in a poignant plea to the One above. And then we recited the *Hallel* prayer. What a *Hallel* it was! Even the walls were crying with emotion, as the Rabbi tried to make peace between Hashem and His children.

We said *Hallel* with broken hearts. It was an historic, moving event. I will remember the Rabbi, the historic maker of peace, for the rest of my life. He felt our pain more than his own. He gave us much-needed encouragement and told us that G-d will have mercy on us. Long after he left the synagogue, we felt the impact of the *Yom HaDin* [Day of Judgement] of Shavuot.

Promptly at eleven, the local peasants, who had made themselves comfortable in Jewish homes, whose windows were boarded up with wood, began to jeer at us and badger us to leave. They drove around, ordering everyone out of the village. Soon policemen with clubs began to physically threaten us and throw us out. What a tumult! The sick were sighing, the children were crying, and packages were everywhere. It was absolute bedlam.

We drove on to Vobolnik, but didn't find other wagons. It seemed the others were far behind us. Despite our experiences, we tried to be happy, to find the joy in the holy day and fulfill the Torah's command, "You shall rejoice in your holiday."

How I yearned to find a house to rest in! As I drifted off to sleep, I thought of *Hallel*, hens, and the police. . . .[155]

The refugees were mainly headed to the towns of Vobolnik and Kupishak, where the Jews had not been driven out. The

---

154. One of the great Rabbinic Luminaries of Lithuania, at the time, Rabbi Atlas was the Rabbi of Shavel.

155. Eizenberg, *Milchomo Shtoib*, Chapter 13, from page 92

edict of expulsion was only until the town of Vobolnik. A small percentage of the Jews headed to distant Riga, Latvia.

As we arrived near Vobolnik, we met hundreds of wagons. The roads were clogged in a huge traffic jam. There were dozens of homeless people just sitting, dazed, and holding their worldly possessions.

As I feared, there were no empty homes in Vobolnik, which was jam-packed with refugees. Every available inch had been taken. We finally rented an empty stall, in a barn, and I was grateful that at least we had a roof over our heads. Next to our stall was a stall filled with horses, who kept us company. I was thrilled, nevertheless, that we wouldn't be driven away too soon.

I unpacked the wagon, settled the children, shook the dust off my coat and headed to the shul, where the refugees met to pray and exchange news. The shul was always the center for Jews, the place of solace.

In the synagogue I again met a friend from Shavel and we spoke. Soon I noticed that the *Beit Midrash* [house of study] had filled, and there was a Rabbi standing and delivering a lecture. The atmosphere was surreal, as everyone was crying and reciting the confession prayers. The Rabbi was chanting, "*Ashamnu*," [we have sinned], and all repeated the words after him. "*Bogadnu, gozalnu*, etc." It appeared just like Yom Kippur.

"What is going on here?" I asked my friend. "Why is the Rabbi giving such a presentation? He is standing before exhausted, broken, dispirited Jews and saying *ashamnu* with them? Is their *teshuvah* [repentance] not yet complete? Do they still need additional repentance? They are driving us out because we are ill and weak, because nobody cares for us, not because we are sinful."

My friend agreed. Yet I soon had second thoughts. "Maybe we are sinners," I said. "When they drive us out, we belong to no one, and they can do whatever they want. We are definitely sinners, the worst in this world."

"No," my friend firmly replied. "We are not sinners. We don't need to say *ashamnu* during such a painful time. Jews need succor and encouragement, not more guilt. Let us consider ourselves like human beings, and not yell and scream that we have sinned."

"The Jewish *krechtz*, or sigh, lies in our *ashamnu*," I said to him. "We say *ashamnu* every day and cry over our situation."

"Not everyone agrees," said my intelligent friend. "Remember the Rabbi that we met this morning? When we said *Hallel*, the Rabbi told us, "children, this will pass. Let us say *Hallel* and praise *Hashem*.' He understood that the unfortunate refugees have to say *Hallel*. Jews need encouragement, not more pain."

In the middle of the speech a man walked into shul and announced, "Let us go to the funeral of those who died on the wagons mid-way."

The speech was abandoned, and we all left the shul to escort those unfortunates to their final rest. They were lying on the wagons, the sick and elderly, the young and frail from Pokroy who did not survive the journey. Everyone was crying as we accompanied the casualties to their grave. On one of the wagons I saw a small child, Surele, who had died in her mother's arms en route. Another wagon contained an elderly man who had cried, "Hashem, See our pain." His *tallis* and *tefillin* were lying next to him. My heart hurts for these Jews, but only for a moment. Soon I began to envy them. At least they were free of their pain and suffering. Nobody will banish them from their hometown anymore.

Soon a young man approached me and asked, "Do you know where I can get a doctor? My father is very weak." But I had no doctor for him. He wanted to hurry to another city and get medical help, but it was hard to pass the traffic choked roads. Hundreds of thousands had been driven out of their homes within 24 hours.

The homeless had abandoned their packages in the middle of the street, and their children sat on them, just waiting. Their lips were dry and they had no more strength to cry. Their poor mothers were running around, trying to find water for their thirsty little ones.

One old woman sat on her bundle, her head resting on a package, as she recited the afternoon mincha prayer. It was already nightfall, and many were on the road to Kupishak.

I went to shul for *Maariv* and saw people standing in groups, discussing their experiences and making travel plans. No one knew what the morrow would bring. The fortunate Jews had wagons, while others had to go by foot. I went back to the stable where I made *kiddush,* and we ate challah washed down with tea. At least we were no longer traveling in a cramped, bumpy wagon. We fell asleep in our clothes, exhausted from our ordeal.

In the morning, the second day of Shavuot, I woke up and felt sore. Every bone in my body hurt. Soon I returned to the synagogue. The Jews of Vobolnik, who had not been driven out, *davened* in the usual manner. There were no arguments about *Hallel* vs. *Kinot.*

During the daytime more refugees arrived. They were in bad shape; the mothers were holding the hungry children, and searching for food. The plight of those who had no food was very bitter indeed.[156]

Kupishak

I realized we had better get out of Vabolnik, as the locals had no use for us. It was too far from a train station, and we needed to travel by wagon. I rented a wagon and we traveled to Kupishak, which was a larger city, more centrally located. I felt more comfortable knowing we had additional options, in case we needed to escape.

I tried to find an apartment in Kupishak, but it was also impossible because over 5,000 homeless people had settled there. Finally we found a small house, which already contained two families. We had no beds, and slept on the floor. Still, it was an improvement over a stall!

The house was in bad shape, infested with mice and rodents. As we slept, the mice crawled over our bodies. Several times, I found mice hiding in my shoes. We were also infested with lice from lack of clean water and the terrible sanitary conditions.

---

156. Eizenberg, *Milchomo Shtoib,* Chapter 14, page 101

The highlight of our days was our trip to the bathhouse where we received soap and warm water to wash ourselves.

During these trying days, as the newcomers milled about, many Rabbanim who arrived delivered lectures in the synagogue without the confessions. Many tried to encourage us and give us hope to tolerate our situation. We began to hope that Nikolai would have a downfall, and that we would finally be allowed to return home.

The Rabbi of Kupishak, Rav Fievelsohn, was a *tzaddik* who stood up for the rights of the homeless. Anytime someone wanted to take advantage of us, we would go to the Rabbi and complain. Like in other places, there were compassionate Jews, and some who mocked us. This war brought out the best, and the worst, in people.

Some of the homeless would ask Lithuanian peasants to go back to their hometowns and bring their possessions from their abandoned homes. They would pay a pretty price for this, but usually the wagons would come back empty, as the homes were looted. My uncle sent a gentile back home, but all he brought back was four empty containers. Another peasant brought an old hat he found. Everything else was gone.

Those Jews who had some money wanted to leave, to go to Minsk, Vitebsk, and Mohilov, [Russia] where there were some opportunities.

One day, two delegates arrived from Petrograd [St. Petersburg], also in Russia. We eagerly welcomed their arrival, hoping to hear good news.

They gathered all the homeless men into the large synagogue, and we stood in rapt silence. One of the men, who wore a straw hat, said to us, "Dear homeless brothers. The Russian generals want to send you papers, to make you sign documents attesting that you left your homes, not because you were driven out, but on your own free will."

We stood, stunned at his suggestion. What audacity! How could they stoop so low?

"Dear brothers, we don't have to tell you how to reply. You know what they did to you – they drove you out of your homes with 24-hour-notice, and your possessions were lost. Your children died on the fields from hunger and weakness. Hundreds of thousands of Jews were left homeless. They had no mercy on the weak and sick. However, Hashem's kindness was evident; He has protected us, and will continue to do so."

"The entire world is protesting against this terrible cruelty. The blood of our murdered ones is crying out from the earth, calling for revenge. Let us show that we are also humans, and we won't kiss their whip. One day they will yet pay for their actions.

"Brothers. Let us not lose our courage. G-d is with us, and justice is with us!"

As one, we all started to shout, "No! We will never sign." Our wounds were opened a new, and we began to cry like children.

A week later the police came bearing papers asking us to sign. Naturally, we all refused. Retribution was not long in coming.

A week later came the sudden order: The homeless Jews were not allowed to travel to the local villages. They were only allowed to go to Siberia or the city of Penza. Only those who ran on their own free will were allowed to stay locally [aside from Petersburg or Moscow].

How would the authorities know who escaped and who were driven out? The police said that those who have passports from the Rasyan and Telzer areas were allowed to stay because the Germans had invaded their territories. However, most of the refugees did not have such passports.

I was from the lucky ones, as I had a passport from Rasyan. I wanted to leave, but to where? The big cities, such as Moscow, were closed and off limits. In the small cities the situation was the same. I chose not to go anywhere hoping I could return home with my family.[157]

We stayed in Kupishak until the 23rd of July, 1915. Suddenly, the situation changed. The Germans defeated the Russians, attacking them in Vobolnik. The shtetl burned down, and the Jews ran off to Dvinsk.

---

157. Ibid. Chapter 15, page 110

Soon the situation became very tense as the Cossacks arrived, ready for bloodshed, and we were terrified. It was time to leave. We went to the train station to buy tickets. Anywhere would be better than our current situation.

The streets looked like a war zone. The dead and the wounded were lying on the ground, near the limbs of dead horses, and the stench was awful. The devoted nurses were trying to care for the seriously wounded, who were groaning in pain. The Red Cross wagons had pulled up, carrying food rations, and medical supplies. A tall, burly Commander shouted, "All civilians must go home immediately! There is no room for civilians on the trains."

From afar, we heard the sound of cannons shooting. The war front was moving closer. Having no choice, we prepared to return home. Overnight the situation worsened: every time we heard a cannon fire we shuddered in fear. People were running around, frantic, desperate to leave. I saw two captive German soldiers being brought to town.

The following day I went to the station to get tickets for my family. I presented myself as a refugee, and succeeded in obtaining the coveted tickets. There were hundreds of people who were all waiting for tickets, but were unable to get them.

Before we left the region, I went to see the Rabbi of Kupishak, Rav Feivelson, and thank him for the kindness he showed us. The German planes were already covering the area, and danger was apparent. The Rabbi was very afraid, and I advised him to leave. But where could he go? He couldn't even get to the train station, as it was dangerous for him to be outside.

The following day, my family and I packed our bags and headed to the train station in a wagon. However, it was impossible to get close due to the throngs of refugees. We remained in our wagon until the evening. The platform manager asked us to leave, because civilians were not allowed to remain in the area.

We searched for shelter in the area, and were directed to a small Jewish home. The owner, a kindhearted man, agreed to take us in, but his wife refused, yelling and cursing at her husband. "I don't want homeless people here, to bring lice into our house!" she shouted.

So, we stayed in the man's barn. The children huddled on the packages, and I walked around in circles until dawn.[158]

At five a.m. we left our "shelter" in the stable and headed to the train station. We were weary and exhausted. We hoped to get onto the platform and secure our seats.

On our way to the station, we saw a terrible sight: a Lithuanian peasant was bringing a half-dead soldier on a small wagon. The soldier's feet were dragging on the ground and the wagon was soaked in blood, which coated the wheels. The poor soldier was writhing in pain, begging for a drink of water, which we gave him but he could not swallow. As they neared the station, the soldier died. I told the peasant to stop the wagon and straighten the poor soldier's legs, which were still dragging on the ground. He tied them with a bit of twine and then continued on his way.

When we arrived at the station, we began to drag our belongings onto the train. I felt fortunate to be aboard. There was a tremendous rush of people, Jews, peasants, and Christians, everyone trying to escape the front lines. We sat in our seats, ate a bit, and felt better.

There were packages of food for the soldiers on the platform: flour, bread, and yeast. There were three trains: two for civilians and one for the Red Cross. Soon the notice arrived stating that only two trains would be allowed to leave that day. Anyone who did not have a ticket was asked to leave. Soon the area was empty of civilians, who left their packages behind. Rabbi Feivelsohn had also sent a wagon with his books to ship to another city, but the wagon arrived too late, and there was no room. His precious books were left, abandoned, at the station.

Finally, the train began to move, and we all sighed with relief. We had barely left the station when we heard a tremendous boom. We later learned that the Russians had exploded the station with dynamite, to prevent its possession by the Germans. All the belongings were destroyed, including Rabbi Feivelsohn's

---

158. Ibid. Chapter 16, Page 122

books. The Rabbi himself had managed to escape with the last train to Dvinsk.

As we continued to travel, we passed fields filled with broken airplanes, and bodies of men and animals lying on the ground. We saw entire villages consumed in flames. No one asked, "Why were we the lucky ones to survive?" Everything that was built up over hundreds of years of toil was consumed by the flames.[159]

Shimon and the Tallit Katan

The author related the following story.

A young Jewish soldier, who identified himself as Shimon Grunzweig from Lupalov, came to town. He was 26 years old, and his face was tanned and weather-beaten from the sun. He looked lonely and unhappy, but was elated to find another Jew.

"I haven't seen any Jews in eight weeks," he told me. After we spoke, he asked me to do him a favor.

"I need a *tallit katan*," he begged. "Can you spare one?"

"But of course," I said. "I can give you a pair of *tefillin*, too."

"I don't need *tefillin*, because I have nowhere to put it. I just need a *tallit katan*," he replied. "I can't go to battle without it. This will be my protection, my guarantee that I will be buried among Jews."

He explained that the Russians buried their casualties in mass graves. However, when they saw a body draped in a *tallit katan*, they knew it was a Jew, and they buried him separately. He had been in the city of Graz back in June and saw entire fields covered with bodies.

I gave him a *tallit katan* and blessed him that he return safely. He became very emotional and said, "My life is not worth much, but at least I will be buried with Jews."

"How does the city look?" I asked him.

"Ah. There are no Jews in Graz anymore. Now the peas-

---

159. Eizenberg, *Milchomo Shtoib*

ants don't have anyone to blame for their troubles. Instead, the soldiers are looting and stealing from the peasants. Sometimes they barge into Jewish homes, eat and drink their fill, and then set piles of straw, burning the houses to the ground. They don't want the treasures and properties to fall into German hands."

Shimon gave me his address in the Mohilev region on the other side of the Dnieper, and begged me to give regards to his parents if I ever see them. He had not seen them since he began his service in the military. "Why don't you write to them?" I asked, "I don't want to write to them, because my life is no life," he said. "I am wandering about, without a day and night, living on the battlefield. If I survive, I will go back home, and if I don't, I won't be too sorry about it. But if you see them, tell them you met me."

Shimon told me that he buried sixty Jewish soldiers near my hometown in June, and put a *Magen David* (Star of David) on their graves. "If you return, please erect a tombstone for them," he said. He also said he doesn't plunder the bodies and take their boots, like the other soldiers.

I parted with him certain I would never see him again. (To my surprise, though, at a later date I met his parents and gave them regards.)

The soldier was very grateful for the *tallis katan* he received. Yet he was nonchalant about his chances of dying on the battlefield. After all he has experienced, life and death were almost the same to him.[160]

Rabbi Yehudah Leib Graubart (1862–1937) known as the Stacheuver Rav was born in Shrensk Poland and became the Rabbi of Stascow, Poland near the German border at the age of 21. In 1915, he was sent to Russia by the regime as a hostage, along with other Rabbis and notable Jews where they were held responsible for other Jews accused of "espionage." In exile, the Rabbi authored a book, *Sefer Zikaron* (Memorial Book) on his experiences and the plight of Jews during the war. After four years, he was returned to Stascow.

---

160. Ibid. pp. 111–115

The following is an excerpt which has been adapted from *Sefer Zikaron*.

Yom Kippur

It was Yom Kippur eve, 5675 [1914], not long before nightfall. A Russian general named Novokow showed up with his troops. I wanted to meet with him, but I wasn't granted permission. Only a military official, a Pole named Sokolowski, who had been appointed the city commissioner, could get in. I asked his permission to deploy the civil guard for their rounds that night, just as they had been doing up until then, and made it clear to him that a guard was necessary because not too long ago soldiers had carried out a pogrom here. He answered that the troops that had arrived weren't thieves, just soldiers. But I asked a second time. He answered me offhandedly, just a word or two, and it wasn't clear to me what he meant – yes or no? – But even so I told him that they should be on guard the entire night.[161]

The next day, during the *Musaf* service,[162] a rumor went around saying that four Jews, advisors to the town hall, had been arrested by the commissioner. I went over there and found out that the commissioner had commanded that they be kept as hostages so that order in the town would be maintained. What order? The [clerks] had no idea. They were clearly embarrassed. I left and approached Sochnowsky, who was deputy to the mayor and asked that he speak to the commissioner about them and try not to make the ransom too high to pay. But he said that he wouldn't go to that "murderer" for any sum in the world and told me that just that morning, when he went to the commissioner with some minor request, Sokolowski grabbed

---

161. Yehudah Leib Graubart, *Sefer Zikaron*, p. 17

162. On Yom Kippur, five major prayers are recited – one in the evening and four during the day. Musaf is the second major prayer of the daytime services. It is the only day of the year to have five major prayers. Other holidays and the Sabbath have four, while weekdays have three.

his rifle and pointed it at him and was poised to shoot. We called a meeting to discuss what we should do, but it ended inconclusively. We returned to the synagogue, and an hour later they were taken to Sandomiertz on the commissioner's order. The women were weeping and wailing, and I was trying to comfort them and calm them down, saying that the danger was past. For, here, in town, who could stop the commissioner from doing any evil? But now that the men were out of his jurisdiction we had time to plead their case, especially because the area official knew these people to be honest and upright citizens.

So now we're back in synagogue and are praying the *Ne'ila* service, even though the day is far from over, but then word of a new tragedy arrived, namely that Jews from the village of Tschigun have been brought [to town]. Before we have a chance to think or do anything, a young boy comes in and shatters our senses with the news that a Jew has been hanged in the street. People pushed out of the synagogue where a heart-wrenching, blood-curdling sight awaited us: a man we all knew, from the village of Tschigun, was hanging from a streetlight. His soul had left his body. The street was deathly silent; not a living being was to be seen. I walked back and forth until I met a Pole who told me that a quarter of an hour earlier, at the edge of the city at the bottom of the hill, Cossacks had shot ten Jews and thrown their bodies into a pit they had dug and then covered with dirt.

My heart in tatters, full of grief and foreboding, I went home. There, in our [living] room, many people were praying. They too heard that Jews had been brought here from the village but they don't know what has happened to them. My young son is surprised by my quiet, and wants to know why I sit and linger instead of running to the commandant's office to plead for their lives. I evade the question and answer that one mustn't be hasty. That night, the wife of one of the murdered men came to see me (he resided in Staszow and had been a prayer leader there) with the same request. I answered her that it would be unwise to go at night. When morning came, the end of the matter would have been heard.[163] All the people were afraid and mourned the losses of the day.[164]

The author explains why eleven Jews were murdered.

On Yom Kippur night, the home of a farmer in the village of Tschigun, some 15 versts[165] from Staszow, caught fire and burned down. In the morning, the woman of the house came to town to ask the doctor at the hospital to treat the burns she received on her hands. She stopped in at the shoemaker, Smolin, and told him what happened to her. He asked her if she suspected anyone of arson. She answered him that she did not suspect anyone. But he continued to ask: "Well, don't some Jews live there?" She answered that there were some Jews living there. When he asked if it was possible that one of them was responsible, she said that there was one Jew who hated her because two weeks earlier she had been together with some Cossacks in his shop in the village when they stole from him. "Well, in that case, it's obvious that the Jew took his revenge on you and burned your house down." The words slowly entered the peasant woman's heart until she nodded her head in agreement. Then the shoemaker told her: "You mustn't tarry. Go to the commandant here in town and lodge a complaint about that Jew, and he'll see that you get justice." So she, even though she knew it was a lie, went with him. He served as her mouthpiece and told the general and the commandant the story as if it were a proven fact. And she decided to go along with it and backed up the story.

When the Russians heard the cry of the oppressed woman, they didn't scorn or reject her pleading, but immediately the

---

163. Paraphrase of Ecclesiastes 12:13, meaning "the truth be emerge soon enough."

164. Graubart, *Sefer Zikaron*, p. 18

165. A Russian measure of length, about .66 mile or 1.1 km.

commander ordered a captain and three Cossacks to ride to the village and bring "the vandal Jew" before him.[166]

So the riders came to the village but didn't find the man they were looking for, because it was the holy day of Yom Kippur and he was praying with a congregation in [a house of prayer located in] a forest some three versts[167] away. He had not been home the night before either since he had stayed there. When the peasant woman's house went up in flames, the Jews were reciting Psalms in a group. When the riders learned where he was, they rode that way, but instead of finding just the one, the riders found eleven Jews wrapped in prayers shawls and wearing white *kittels*,[168] immersed in prayer, and so it seemed contemptible in their eyes to lay hand on that individual alone[169] and therefore commanded the men to come to town with them. The owner of the house of prayer, the agent Moshe Edelstein, prepared a feast for them and even hired two wagons for the people and took a bundle of money with him, and they left. When they came to town, the wagons stopped in front of the post office, where the general had set up shop, and the Cossacks surrounded them. The captain went in and came out after five minutes, whereupon he gave the command in the general's name: the Jew – about whom the peasant woman had complained – was to be hanged on the tree in a street right there in the city, while the other ten were not to be hanged but merely shot to death, and not in public but outside city limits. It took all of ten minutes to carry out the meticulous sentences.[170]

In the morning, the wives of the dead came to town carry-

---

166. Graubart, *Sefer Zikaron*, p. 18

167. A Russian measure of length, about .66 mile or 1.1 km

168. A *kittel* is a burial shroud. It is customary for Jewish men in the Ashkenazi tradition to wear the *kittel* on solemn occasions, such as Yom Kippur, Passover night, when standing under the marriage canopy, etc.

169. Paraphrase on Esther 3:5 in the context of Haman's plan to exterminate the entire Jewish people instead of merely seeking revenge against Mordechai, his adversary: ". . . it seemed contemptible in his eyes to lay a hand on Mordechai alone, for they had made known to him the people of Mordechai."

170. Graubart. *Sefer Zikaron*, p. 19

ing their husbands' overcoats, because the Cossacks had taken the men away coatless, in a rush. The wife of the hanged man also carried a certificate issued by the village council saying her husband was an honest, upright individual and not a suspect in any way in the fire at the peasant woman's house. Just imagine the scene of horror when the women were informed of the fate that had just befallen them. The pen is useless, the scribe a liar, when attempting to describe the scene. The women fainted again and again, beat their heads, tore at their hair, fell to the floor. Their cries rose to the heavens and everything around was soaked in dread.[171]

Rabbi Graubart republished an article from the Hebrew journal, "Ha'Ivri" (The Hebrew) which described the sufferings of Jews during the war. Excerpts of the article are contained below.[172]

About the Travails of the Jews during the War

Poles had falsely testified that a synagogue was full of explosives, buried there by the Jews to help the Germans. One Sabbath, during the Musaf prayer service, the synagogue was surrounded by armed soldiers and an officer, accompanied by his adjutants, who soon entered. A thorough search ensued. When the officer reached the *bima*,[173] underneath which the furnace was located, he saw the wicket [door] that covered the heater. He pulled back sharply and ordered his soldiers to open it. But they also pulled back sharply, too afraid to approach the place of danger. So the officer commanded the synagogue sexton to open the wicket. But the furnace hadn't been in use all summer long, so the wicket had rusted and could not be opened. This made the military officer even more suspicious, and he was close to giving the order to kill all the Jews there, had there not been a miracle just then and pliers and hammers were brought and the wicket

---

171. Ibid. p. 20
172. *Ha'ivri*, 5676 (1916), issues 25, 26; Mr. Mordechai Katz
173. A raised prayer platform.

was finally opened. First, the officer ordered the sexton to climb down, and then he sent his soldiers to follow, and finally went down himself. When he didn't find anything down there, he cursed the Poles and the Jews alike, ordered the congregation expelled, and had his horses brought in instead.[174]

In another incident, armed soldiers surrounded the home of a rabbi in the middle of the night, and an officer entered the home, woke him, and ordered him to follow him to the synagogue. The rabbi's wife began to cry but the officer threatened her with his sword and thereby silenced her. At the synagogue, the officer told the rabbi he would carry out a search in the rabbi's presence, and if he found a telephone connected to the enemy camp, about which reliable sources had informed him that such a telephone was there, then he would cut the rabbi's head off with his sword. The rabbi was terrified, what if the Poles had actually set up a telephone there as a plot against the Jews. He started to recite the *Vidui* deathbed confession under his breath . . . The miracle occurred, no telephone was found and the rabbi was released.[175]

---

174. *Ha'ivri*, quoted from Graubart, p. 264
175. Ibid.

Chapter 4

Under German Occupation

Warsaw under Siege

The luminary, **Rabbi Yitzchak Zev Soloveitchik,** from Brisk was in Warsaw during the German aerial bombardment. As the Germans attacked, Rabbi Soloveitchik went down to the basement for cover as everyone else did. However, when the noise suddenly increased and explosions became more thunderous, he immediately arose and returned to his apartment. Others present later wondered about his behavior. He was in less danger in the basement, but when it became even more dangerous, he went up to his apartment on the top floor.

The rabbi responded that a person must have complete faith in all situations that G-d will protect; however, the Rambam (Maimonides) writes a person should not put himself in a situation where a miracle will be needed. Thus, earlier when the explosions were lighter, the refuge in the basement which was built for such a bombardment was sufficient. But once the explosions intensified, the shelter would not help, so there was no difference between being inside or outside the shelter.[176]

In December, 1914, the Russians managed to keep the German advance out of Warsaw, but the Germans forced the Russian abandonment on August 5, 1915. At the time, the Germans occupied Central Poland and Lithuania, with a population of two million Jews.

---

176. Quoted from *Tallilei Orot*, (Collection of Commentaries on the Torah) on *Parashat VaYetze* Volume II, p. 11

The predicament of the Jews of Warsaw mirrored other cities in the region which were overcrowded and lacked adequate provisions. By September, 1915, about half of the Jews within the Czarist Empire were living under German occupation.

The German occupation of Warsaw initially brought hope among the Jewish population. Perhaps the suffering and starvation would end under new control. Upon the German capture of Warsaw, a Yiddish daily, *The Ilustrirte Velt*, wrote that "the Jewish community will now regain itself."[177]

The *Ober Ost* (German high command) sought the cooperation of the local Jewish communities. One German appeal in Yiddish to Polish Jews stated:

> The gates of life have been closed to you; it is now your power to open them. Jews of Poland! The hour of reckoning has come. The heroic armies of the great powers, Germany, Austria, and Hungary are in Poland, and will, with the help of G-d, avenge your oppressors and persecutors.[178]

The loyalty of the Poles was also sought. On Nov, 5, 1916, the Germans proclaimed a quasi-independent State of Poland. But as requisitions for food supplies continued where items were sparse, the support by the Poles diminished.

The German occupation was laden with regulations. They forced many civilians to work in munitions and other factories, and often kept them in internment camps. They issued numerous prohibitions. One such ruling was an ordinance prohibiting Jews from wearing, "long Eastern coats." Many Jews refused, and suffered reprisals with heavy fines. The Germans also extracted money with threats of imprisonment.[179]

As the German army continued to advance eastward, additional horrors awaited many refugees who crowded into cities in the Ober

---

177. Herzl Book, Volume 7, January, 1971, p. 204
178. *LJC*, November 20, 1914, p. 15
179. *LJC*, January 20, 1915, p. 13

Ost.[180] The lack of supplies resulted in starvation and disease. Shortages of food were due to the hardships of war. Other factors causing shortages were the poor harvest in Germany in the prior year along with the termination of food imports from Russia. Supplies from distant sources were stopped due to the Entente blockade of Germany. Following the German incursion into Poland, the German army requisitioned local supplies and the people faced shortages which caused prices to spike.

The Jews being a disproportionate number of homeless were severely impacted.

The situation worsened over time. Under the leadership of General Erich Von Ludendorff, the Germans confiscated enormous amounts of supplies. Between 1916 and 1917, they seized four-fifths of the potatoes from Lithuania, six-sevenths of the cattle, and almost all the butter and eggs. The Germans took apart factories, and even sent church bells back to Germany.[181]

The New York Times reported on the desperate situation – "Thousands Starve to Death in Poland," November 30, 1915.

"Hundreds of thousands of the civil population in the Warsaw district of Poland are suffering for want of food. A considerable percentage of this number, still are homeless living in huts, caves and abandoned trenches."[182]

According to the report, there were, "acute food shortages," with "prices rising," and the "fear that importation would cease altogether."[183]

The destruction of war caused a flood of refugees into Warsaw. Many were drifting back into Warsaw under German control.[184]

"In Warsaw and Lodz women now rise at 3:00 o'clock in the morning to get good places in the bread lines and not miss the chance

---

180. The Ober-Ost was the area in Eastern Europe under German occupation during the war.

181. Piotr S. Wandycz, *Land of Partitioned Poland*, (1795–1918), University of Washington Press, Seattle, 1975, pp. 340–341

182. *NYT*, "Thousands Starve to Death in Poland," November 30, 1915, p. 3

183. Ibid.

184. Ibid.

to obtain some food at least." The situation worsened by shortages of coal due to destruction of mines, and inadequate railway facilities.[185]

According to the report, the Germans were assisting both Jews and Christians with at least 82 soup kitchens in Warsaw. However, such efforts did not sufficiently ameliorate the suffering.[186]

The inevitable result of starvation ensued with disease and epidemics. A *New York Times* quote estimated that 250,000–300,000 people in Warsaw alone were being supported by outside assistance.[187]

"The greatest need is for fats, butter, rice, and beans. The Citizen's Committee asserts that all flour, corn and feed materials have been confiscated by the military authorities or taken to Prussia."[188]

German claims to making efforts to feed the civilian populations could not be supported by the extent of the suffering. Just following the capture of Warsaw, "The German government has given assurances that 80% of what has been taken will be returned when milled. The Germans have taken charge of the potato crop which they declare is being given exclusively to the civilian population in districts not occupied by the military. Exportations from one district to another are forbidden. The Germans are importing some flour, rye and salt and small quantities of coal into Poland."[189]

Other accounts describe the horrors of Warsaw in those days.

Sammy Gronemann (1875–1952), the son of an Orthodox rabbi who grew up in Danzig Germany, was a lawyer, Zionist activist, and writer, who served on the Eastern Front during the war. He noted, "The hardships and pain of these 300,000 Warsaw Jews, I can hardly speak about because my words won't do justice to the horrors that have befallen our brothers here in Poland."[190]

He added, "Yesterday I was at a *cheder* that houses 1,000 kids with only 25 teachers. Not a single kid has something decent to wear, full

---

185. Ibid.
186. Ibid.
187. Ibid.
188. Ibid.
189. Ibid.
190. Sammy Gronemann, *Hawdalah un Zaphemstreich*, Judisher Verlag Konigstein, Berlin, 1924, p. 77

of rags and ripped pieces of clothing. It was a horrible sight to see. The teacher's salary is only 11 ruble a month."[191]

In a letter from Warsaw quoted from Reuters news service: "Death from starvation is a real fact. It is witnessed in every house. Jewish mothers feel happy to see their nursing babies die and end their suffering. Our wealthiest people cut and sell their hair, so they may be able to buy necessities of life, like bread, for their dying children."[192]

M. Ferbenstein, President of the Polish Zionist Organization, reported that "70,000 children in Warsaw are beggars. Daughters of some of the best families have been forced to lead an immoral life for the purpose of obtaining food for their parents at the German barracks; The very old and young are fast disappearing altogether."[193]

The following is from a story entitled, "The Churban (destruction) of Warsaw."

> The horrors of ill-fated Warsaw are so appalling that no pen is powerful enough to describe them adequately. New *Kinot* [Lamentations] would have to be written to express the terrible weight that is bearing down upon the great Jewish community and crushing it to the point of annihilation. Here is a part of it.
>
> "Death by starvation no longer has an abstract meaning. We see it here, everywhere at the street corner, in every alley, in every hovel. It stalks the highways and the byways."[194]
>
> "Our best people are cutting their daughters' hair to buy bread for starving babies. . . ."[195]
>
> "Our soup kitchens must be kept going somehow. Three thousand babies depend upon them to keep them barely alive. The parents try to find a crust somewhere – they have to relinquish their places in the bread line to the children who are falling victim to hunger and typhoid. Help us! Arouse America! She is our only hope! If she fails us, we are lost!"[196]

---

191. Ibid.
192. *LJC*, August 17, 1918, p. 8
193. *American Jewish Chronicle*, March 22, 1918, p. 531
194. *Canadian Jewish Chronicle*, August 17, 1917, p. 7
195. Ibid.
196. Ibid.

Vilna

Following the German entry into the Lithuanian capital of Vilna on Yom Kippur, September 18, 1915, its legendary Jewish community was relieved of Russian control but the travails continued.

In his book *Hawdalah un Zaphenstreich* (Havdalah and Tatoos), Gronemann described the poverty, unsanitary conditions, starvation and disease in Vilna.

> Awful are those courtyards that are filled with tons of garbage and the people sat closely to each other. They sit on dirty steps leading down from the courtyard to literally ditches, void of air and light without a trace of furniture. Whole families sit in these places. Women that don't have enough rags to cover themselves to go outside; people, on account of the dirt and miserable conditions have become completely blind. I know of a family that only survived because their 6 year old daughter begged for food the entire day and then brought it home.[197]

The Faces

Gronemann continued . . .

> Outside in front of the door sits an elderly lady with fiery eyes warming her hands on a bucket of coals. Behind her sits a little girl that through the shade looks very creepy and almost like an animal. But the faces! Everywhere you look you see faces that tell stories of a whole nation. The fate of these people, are one! How many kinds of poor people are there!
>
> Suddenly you hear from afar a terrible cry from an 8-year-old girl like a wounded animal. There lies a mother with two kids in the snow screaming to high heaven, "Please have mercy on me, *nebbich*, (pity) see how I and my kids are rolling here in the snow." The word, "*nebbich*," doesn't fit the description of what

---

197. Sammy Gronemann, *Hawdalah un Zaphenstreich*, Judisher Verlag: Konegstein, Berlin, 1924, p. 73

I saw. A fourteen-year-old girl stands around, covering her hair with a scarf whispering for charity. Everybody gives but we all know it's just prolonging the inevitable.

In front of me walks a young man who suddenly staggers and falls. People around are immediately gathering to carry him to the nearest house. This is everyday life. Women always carry pieces of sugar with them to revive the fainted.[198]

The Feldrabbiner

In 1915, sixteen German rabbis were sent east to assist the troops and administer to the needs of Jewry under German occupation. They also acted as intermediaries between the Jewish populations and the German authorities.

One such rabbi, Leopold Rosenak, frequently interacted with the Ostjuden, (Eastern Jews) some of whom turned to him for help obtaining firewood, warm clothing, and for counsel in dealing with issues of marriage and divorce. He issued pamphlets in German and Yiddish to prevent the spread of Cholera and other diseases. He often managed to obtain provisions from the German army. He was decorated on numerous occasions by the Germans for his service. In 1916, he received the Iron Cross 2nd Class.[199]

In 1918, there were 900 soup kitchens in Eastern Europe under the German occupation. About 15,000 school children received daily hot meals. Much of the relief was provided by American Jews and obtained by Hilfsverein (German Jewish Aid Society) in neutral countries.[200] Rabbi Rosenak's contacts around the world helped provide shipments of food supplies. Through personal negotiations with Holland, he was able to obtain fruits and vegetables for two consecutive years.[201] When his congregation asked him to return in September, 1917, he responded that he could not leave the suffer-

---

198. Ibid.

199. Minnie Rosenak, *The Rosenaks of Bremmen: Father and Son: A Chapter of German Jewish History*, Jerusalem, 1988, p. 19

200. Ibid. p. 20

201. Ibid. p. 21

ing masses. He suggested that it is a privilege for the Congregation whose rabbi was serving in the cause of such vital work.[202]

Following the *Shmini Atzeret* holiday in 1917, he described the suffering he witnessed in the city of Bialystok, Poland, in a letter to his family.

> On Simchas Torah the poor Jewish women and their children and infants pressed forward in the synagogue in an unstoppable stream, pushing toward my place and calling out for bread. It was a deeply affecting moment which began to cause concern with all the crowding and screaming. I went to the lectern and in front of the open ark of the Torah, I promised them to take the necessary steps immediately."[203] Rabbi Rosenak wrote about how he went to the mayor of the city and managed to obtain bread and herring for five to six thousand people from the military authorities.[204] He adds, "This morning an infant boy was found in front of the hospital with a note asking he be raised as a Jew.[205]

On April 7, 1916, another German field rabbi, Aron Tanzer, wrote about how he raised funds to organize a tea coach which goes through the streets and gives out tea with sugar to the poor. "May 10, 1916. . . . In Berlin I met with the Gentlemen from the East committee and received from young Mr. Cohn another 5,000 Mark for the *cheder*, so that I have 20,000 Mark at my disposition. . . . Pesach is without *matzos* for most poor people here and otherwise sad. It can only be explained because of this misery that some public kitchens opened to give out *chometz*, 13,000 meals daily.[206]

Rabbi Tanzer arrived at the city of Brest-Litovsk where he would be devoting much of his time at service, "I will always be haunted by the terrible experience of entering the immense burning and smok-

---

202. Ibid. p. 16
203. Ibid. p.17
204. Ibid.
205. Ibid.
206. Arnold (Aron) Tanzer Leo Baeck Institute, AR485/MF 705, January 2006

ing heap of rubble, which only a few days earlier had been a great and thriving city."[207] As other Feldrabbiner, he established a soup kitchen, "There was a great lack of food in the city near the front, the little food that was available was sold at exorbitant prices and so the poor suffered the most. When I arrived there in 1915, I established a "Kitchen for the People" from the money of the "Help Association of German Jews" and with the support of the military headquarters.

Poor travelers were able to stay at a house that was on the property of the synagogue. It had 80 beds with an attached kitchen and "was used very frequently and the poor received free board. The Jewish Communal Kitchen served 500 free lunches a day. Bikur Cholim (society that visits the sick) took care of the "needs of the sick widows, orphans and poor and supported them in a noble and sufficient way."

He added, "Whoever experienced this gruesome picture of devastation will never forget it."[208]

The German occupation forces deemed it important to provide an education for Jewish children that included secular subjects. One of the rabbis, Joseph Carlebach, was delegated the task of organizing an educational system for Jews under German occupation in the Lithuanian city of Kovno. The rabbi devised a program based upon the model of *Torah Im Derech Eretz*, "Torah Education with the Ways of the Land," originally formulated by the sage, Rabbi Samson Rafael Hirsch, 1808–1888, which emphasized a strong religious education along with secular studies, as he also consulted with local rabbinical leaders and received their support. The relatively small school, soon grew as parents placed their trust in Rabbi Carlebach. After one year, there were one thousand students.[209] The Rabbi was also partially responsible for the reopening of the famed Slobodka Yeshiva which was closed due to the ravages of the war. Rabbi Rosenak was also involved in the reopening of the famed Slobodka Yeshiva. At the re-opening ceremony in the presence of German military officers on January

---

207. David Fine, *Jewish Integration in the German Army in the First World War*, Walter De Gruyter, Berlin/Boston, 2012, p. 188

208. Leo Baeck Institute, AR485/MF 705, January 2006

209. Rav Shlomo Carlebach, *Ish Yehudi: The Life and Legacy of a Torah Giant: Rav Joseph Tzvi Carlebach*, Shearit Joseph Publications, New York, 2008, pp. 117–118

31, he noted the Yeshiva's previous state of disarray due to the war. Funds for the project were raised by German Jewish communities.[210]

A German Rabbi who served in Lithuania, Leo Deutschlander, established an extensive Jewish network of schools known as Yavneh.[211] He also established a school system for girls under German auspices with the help of a young seamstress Sara Schenirer, which was known as "Bais Yaakov." The purpose was to counter the secularization of Jewish girls due to the war as well as their inability to earn a living during the war which sometimes led to a moral decline.[212] Such efforts were also supported by the Hilfsverein, the KfoD, Agudas Yisroel, and the German government.

Words of Protest

Rabbi Joseph Carlebach, who lived from 1883–1942, was a German military rabbi, scholar and scientist. In 1912, he earned a PhD, and in 1914, received rabbinic ordination from the luminary Rabbi Tzvi Dovid Hoffmann. On September 15, 1917, the Saturday night before Rosh Hashanah, his words evoked a powerful message, expressing his views on the war and those who bore responsibility for the immense suffering.

On that night, Rabbi Carlebach preached at the synagogue Ohel Yaakov in Kovno. Jews converged upon the synagogue to hear the words from the esteemed scholar and leader. The German commanders insisted that the German-Jewish soldiers sit on one side of the synagogue, Russian Jewish soldiers (prisoners of war) on the other and in between them, the local Jews.

He stunned the audience which expected to hear words in support of his native Germany. He began with commonly heard words in German circles, "We did not want this war," which was a phrase often used by Germans to imply that Germany's enemies, the En-

---

210. Carlebach, *Ish Yehudi*, pp. 117–118 Also see American Jewish Chronicle, March 1, 1916, p. 20

211. *Ish Yehudi*, Ibid.

212. Pearl Benisch, *Carry Me in Your Heart: The Life and Legacy of Sarah Schenirer*, Feldheim, New York, 2003, p. 9

tente, drew her reluctantly into the conflict. But the rabbi's implied message was far different; that no one in that room wanted this destructive war, for which Germany bore much of the responsibility. Rabbi Carlebach did not absolve Germany from its responsibility for the war and its resulting carnage.

The rabbi praised the level of Torah study in the Eastern territories and stated that German Jews had much to learn from the Eastern Jewry. He mentioned how German Jewish soldiers were learning Torah from local Jews. He also stated that it was symptomatic that Jews from different sides sat together in synagogue, separated by a German ruling, prohibited from mingling.[1]

The Alter of Slobodka

Rabbi Natan Tzvi Finkel, the *Rosh Yeshiva* of the famed Slobodka Yeshiva was in Germany when the war broke out and as a Russian citizen, he was taken prisoner. One of the German guards gave special attention to R' Natan Tzvi and looked over him, making sure that he was provided with all his needs and that no harm befell him. At the end of the war, the soldier revealed his Jewish identity to him and went to learn in Slobodka. Because of the suspicion that his assistance could have aroused against the esteemed rabbi, he did not reveal his own Jewish identity in order to protect him. He joked, that before R' Natan became the *mashgiach* (supervisor) over him, he was the *mashgiach* over R' Natan.[2]

---

1. Parts were found in "Voices of Opposition to the First World War among Jewish Thinkers" by Rivka Horowitz. Leo Baeck Institute, Vol. XXXIII, 1988, p. 254. NOTE: Rabbi Carlebach was executed by the Nazis near Riga on March 26, 1942. His wife and younger children also perished in the holocaust.

2. Dovid Katz, *Tenuat HaMussar*, Feldheim, Jerusalem, 2001, Vol. 3 p. 59

Chapter 5

Encounters

When the German army pressed into Poland, German Jewish soldiers came into contact with their fellow Jews from Eastern Europe. The encounters were a clash of cultures. Germany was considered a cultured and advanced society where its Jews had been striving for equality for over a century. Most German Jews were immersed in their surrounding culture, while much of Eastern Jewry was confined to an insular existence under Czarist rule.

The Ostjuden (Jews of the east), under Czarist rule, lacked the lifestyle emancipation had offered western European Jewry and to a larger extent remained entrenched in the world of traditional Judaism. Their Judaism was an integral part of their being. It was a world most German Jews had long forgotten after decades of assimilation. Many German Jewish soldiers, considered their encounters more of an annoyance and an embarrassment. They preferred not to associate with the Ostjuden whom they perceived as backwards for their adherence to tradition, and unaesthetic due to the manner in which they were dressed and groomed. To the Germans they appeared ill mannered due to different cultural norms of protocol and behavior.

One German Jewish soldier who was a renowned scholar of the romance languages, recalled that his encounter with the Ostjuden initially left him shaken and that the cultural gap between himself and Ostjuden confirmed for him his Germanness, "I could not be anything but a German."[3]

---

3. Victor Klemperer, Curriculum, p. 484, quoted from War Land and the East-

To the Eastern Jew, the German Jew appeared foreign. He dressed like a German, possessed German mannerisms, and spoke German as a first language. The Yiddish term, *Daitcher* meaning "German" was commonly used in reference to a non-observant, beardless, more worldly, assimilated Jew. The German Jew was more orderly, the Ostjude was far less concerned with detail. The German was punctual the Eastern Jew was often not. A popular joke related the story of a Jew from Kovno who was told to make an appointment with the German rabbi during his consultation hours: "I can speak with G-d by day and night and with the German army rabbi I must make an appointment?"[4]

Eastern European Jews were aghast when German rabbis, accustomed to Western models of religious decorum insisted that children be prevented from entering synagogues "in order not to disturb the service."[5]

By 1916, Jewish German soldiers were already in Poland for over a year and a half and they saw the suffering of the Ostjuden. They saw that despite all travails, the Ostjuden remained devoted to G-d; that they were festive and happy at their synagogues. Many German Jewish soldiers only saw their humiliation and did not sense the beauty and depth of their traditions which seemed so distant from them. However, some found within the Ostjuden an inner spirituality. For them, it was an examination into their own self-image as Jews; a self-discovery of their own Jewishness. Some were inspired and deeply impressed by the piety and sense of solidarity of the Ostjuden. They were also impressed by the hospitality bestowed upon them by their fellow Jews.

Arnold Zweig (1887–1968) was a German writer who over time became a vocal critic of the war. He initially volunteered for active duty. In 1920, he authored "The Face of Eastern European Jewry" which evoked sympathy for the Ostjuden. After the war, he became

ern Front, Vejas Gabriel Liulevicius, Cambridge University Press, 2000, p. 41

4. Steven E. Auscheim, *Brothers and Strangers: The East European Jew in German and German Jewish Consciousness*, University of Wisconsin Press, 1982, p. 152, quoted from Zionist satirical journal Schlemiel, no. 1 (1919), p. 355

5. Auscheim, *Brothers and Strangers*, p 152, quoted from "Ein Gottesdienst im Osten," AZdJ 81, no. 30 (July 27, 1917), p. 355.

an active socialist Zionist in Germany. Zweig bemoaned the decline of Judaism among German Jewry amid the modern world of European culture, while offering high praise of the Ostjuden.

> We know that our forefathers were relatives of the men we find today in the cities of Lithuania, Poland and Galicia. . . . Thus, today we speak different languages, think different thoughts, live a different kind of Judaism, eat different dishes, and we have traded part of our soul with Europe, giving up part of our Jewishness.[6]

According to Zweig, the Jews of Western Europe traveled, "a rose colored, enlightened path of a cultural decline into *mishmash* [confusion.]"[7]

Zweig noticed that faith trumps fear and poverty among Eastern European Jews. He also noted how the Ostjuden accepted their lot and how they were devoted to the Sabbath, prayer, and the Torah's commandments. He noticed the sense of unity within the community and that there was no despair: they accepted all that happened as the will of G-d. "Their learning, observance, devotion to G-d were not influenced by idols of East or West."[8]

Hermann Cohen 1842–1918 was a prominent German Jewish Philosopher, who wrote of his impressions of the Eastern Jew for the contemporary German journal *Der Jude*.

Cohen likewise noted the inner strength of the Ostjuden.

> We should have found comfort from his creative power during his suffering and that much real Judaism was still alive in him. His superhuman strength in suffering, his sharp intelligence and immediate capacity will sharpen us and draw us to a spiritual competition.[9]

---

6. Arnold Zweig, *The Face of East European Jewry*, University of California Press, Berkley and Los Angeles, 2004, p. 1

7. Ibid. p. 2

8. Ibid. p. 14

9. Der Jude, Hermann Cohen, "Der Polnische Jude," June, 1916, p. 150

Renowned author and philosopher, Franz Rosenzweig was inspired by an experience at Yom Kippur services in an Orthodox synagogue in Poland.

In May, 1918, Rosenzweig was sent by the German army to an officers' training center in Rembertow near Warsaw, where he came in personal contact with the local Polish Jews. It was a life changing experience for him. From Rembertow, he penned the following letter to his mother.

> I can well understand why the average German Jew no longer feels any kinship with these East European Jews: actually, he has very little kinship left; he has become Philistine, bourgeois; but I, and people like me should feel this kinship strongly.[10]

Written on May 28, 1918, he described the singing in a Hasidic Shtiebel upon a visit to Warsaw on a Saturday evening, to his mother. "These people don't need an organ, with their surging enthusiasm, the voices of children and old men blended. . . . Nor have I ever heard such praying. I don't believe in all that talk about "decadence:" those who now find all this decadent would have seen nothing but decadence even a hundred and fifty years ago."[11]

Rabbi Jacob Sonderling, born in 1878 in Germany, left for the United States in 1924. He later became a founder and congregational leader of the Fairfax Temple in Los Angeles. As one of the Feldrabbiner, Rabbi Sonderling related:

> Here, for the first time, I met people who did not try to give a definition of what they are. . . . They are Jews who did not need sermons to be reminded of their Jewishness. Here I found spiritual knowledge not restricted to professionals, or dignity and inner-independence. . . . Here I was accepted as a Jew without attribution.[12]

---

10. Nahum Glatzer, *Franz Rosenzweig, His Life and Thought*, Hackett Publishing Company, Indianapolis, Ind., 1998, p. 74

11. Ibid. p. 75

12. PhD 97 JS Papers, American Jewish Archive, Cincinnati, OH. p. 97

German Orthodox Jews were also impacted by their encounters. Rabbi Joseph Carlebach stated, "When we stand before a Jew of the East, his mannerisms may be different, as poor as he may be, he can be simple, less hygienic, he may be all these things, but he has an inner superiority when he faces this whole group of Western Jews, of the highest technology but also of the highest depravity."[13]

Letter from the front, June 22, 1915

The following is a letter from an observant German Jewish soldier to his parents:

> I came from the front from Kalvaria. I had seen the destroyed cities of East Prussia and wandered through land that was as devoid of people and animals as Sodom and Gomorrah used to be. Only skeletons of horses were lying left and right on the street. Later I learned about the Jewish suffering in Russia, where Russians arrested Jews for months, and incited pogroms. I heard canons every day and saw the long trains of the wounded. The picture of suffering was in my soul when I entered the synagogue for services. The people were festive, peaceful as if there was no war and praised G-d who makes us content every day. They say he gives us peace. Don't they know about the murdering in Galitzia and Poland where the old and babies are not spared? Don't they feel that it's not a time of blessings but of curses? That G-d punishes rather than makes happy. Don't they feel that? I pray with a sad soul and know that G-d won't listen to my supplications. Then I heard (*ki lekach tov natati lachem . . .*)[*] and remembered that religion does not dissolve suffering, but that it enhances and purifies moral feelings and that we can go through times of trial.[14]

---

13. Quoted from Julius Berger "Zionismus in Polen:" Der Jude November, 1917, pp. 291–299

14. Eugen Tannenbaum, *Kreigsbriefe Deutcherund Osterreicher Juden*, Berlin Neuer Verlag, 1915

The following is an excerpt from Gronemann's book *Hawdalah und Zapfensteich* (Havdalah and Tattoos) in which he relates his experiences in Poland and Lithuania under German occupation. Gronemann details his impressions of the synagogues and houses of study in the East. Here too, as other authors relate, joy is expressed in the everyday life of the Jew despite all hardships.

> Since I have been here in Kovno, I have no desire to go back to the kind of synagogues to which I am accustomed in Germany. Whether Conservative [referring here to the Orthodox] or Reform, I feel uneasy with their orderly, even serene like a military regulated way of praying. I loathe when I see them standing up to take out the Torah scroll like a battalion in formation, so stiff while the rest of the congregation is whispering incoherently. In the East, it is very different.
>
> First of all, the *bimah* [platform], upon which the Torah is read, is in the middle of the room where the Chazzan is standing and his voice fills the room. How could they [in Germany] take such a beautiful center piece of a synagogue away from its true place?
>
> Another big difference; unlike other synagogues where the leader stands apart from the congregation, here the chazzan stands in the middle of the room and leads the prayers upwards like a child begging his father through weeping and song.
>
> The room is filled with people wrapped in their *talleisim* (prayer shawls) swaying back and forth, immersed in prayer, crying out intensely to the One above. The leader wears the *tallis* completely over his head, one can't even see his face. Even somebody who doesn't understand a word is moved. One must be there at the moment to appreciate the fervor.[15]

Gronemann Describes the House of Study

The Western [German] Jew who values order won't appreciate the sight in the *Bet Midrash* [House of Study]. Everyone

---

15. Gronemann, *Hawdalah and Zippenstreich*, p. 73

is minding their own business without taking the next person into account. Some are debating loudly over a passage in the Talmud while others are discussing everyday matters. One elderly man is pacing while talking to himself, kids fight or play running around the *bimah*. The old man screaming as he runs after them. Then one hears shouts from the ladies' section to leave their kids alone. In short, something very different to what I am accustomed to seeing. On the wall, there is a large sign "Spitting Permitted" – something commonly done!

Gronemann's Description of *Simchat Torah* Celebration

Now consider the scene on *Simchat Torah*. Everyone dances with the scrolls in hand, jumping around with closed eyes. It is a sight to see the kids jump and scream all around on the benches on the *bimah*. It appears like they have multiplied themselves by tens! So I asked; why are these people dancing? Why are they happy? What is this Torah that they celebrate? Could you imagine people from a western nation loving their book of laws so much![16]

Gronemann's Meeting with the Gerrer Rebbe

Gronemann discussed his meeting with the Chassidic leader, the Gerrer Rebbe, Rabbi Mordechai Alter, which took place in the city of Crakkow during the German occupation.

Eight o'clock *Shabbos* morning we walk to Panska Street 20 where the Gerrer Rebbe plus thirty other refugee rabbis were gathered. The Rebbe's room nearby was about twice my size with three hundred people standing in the room which was extremely dense and overfilled! Outside, one thousand people were standing in the hallway until outside the house, and nobody was budging to let us in. The *gabbai* [synagogue sexton], under the strict instructions of the rebbe, brought us in pushing and shoving people aside on the way. Once there, the air was

---

16. Gronemann, *Hawdalah and Zippenstreich*, p. 74

so thick I could have cut it myself and when we were called up to the Torah I had no idea how we would get there and how we would get back.[17]

At first the author gives the picture of a chaotic scene and then he continues with the words:

But it was an experience of a lifetime![18]

The following illustrates the cultural divide between observant Jews in the East and West while also pointing out their common bonds.

German POW Camp

On one Yom Kippur in 1917, in a German prisoner of war camp, German and Russian Jews prayed together, bridging cultural differences between them.

Dr. Yaakov Wygodski was a Jewish leader and Zionist activist from Vilna. Imprisoned for a year for participation in protests against the German occupation, and interned in the Czersk POW camp, described his visit to the synagogue of a German POW camp in Zele for *Kol Nidrei* prayers.

Dozens of German Jewish civilians and some Jewish German soldiers occupied the first benches in the upper eastern sections. All remaining benches were occupied by Jewish Russian POW soldiers in their much overused army clothes, with gray-striped trousers, and stripes on the left sleeve indicating the status of prisoner-of-war.

Wygodski was the only civilian prisoner at the service, and so as not to be taken for a German Jew [according to the seating arrangement, no one wanted to seat next to a civilian prisoner], he gave up sitting in the front section and sat together with the military prisoners of war.

---

17. Ibid. p. 75
18. Ibid.

As described by other accounts earlier, Wygodski was also touched by the more passionate tone and free expression of emotions in the prayers of the Eastern European Jews. In Wygodski's words, "The prayers of German Jews have a collective character, while Polish-Lithuanian Jews' prayers have a more individual character!"

At *Kol Nidrei*, a burly Jewish artillery sub-officer, about 30 years old, from a Polish shtetl, covered by a long, heavy custom-made *tallit*, was standing near Wygodski.

He was distressed over the German customs.

Dear Dr. Wygodski, tell me is this a way to pray? Is this our holy Yom Kippur?

"German prayers are slightly different from ours," he answered, trying to calm him: "Their way of praying is not so bad!"

His words failed to assuage him.

Gevalt! Gevalt! For you to say this!" The soldier replied, "Their prayers, God forgive me for what I am about to say, have no real emotion! You and I, when we pray, we tremble during *Kol Nidrei*, even a fish in the water would tremble! When someone comes into our synagogue, he immediately feels a sense of terror, of fear! In our synagogue, when we cry, the cry is the cry of a tormented Jewish heart and rises to the heaven! We take our *Kol Nidrei* very seriously!

As he spoke he wildly waved his hands as if throwing away something distasteful.

He continued, "If you want to talk loudly or groan as an expression of your tormented soul, the pleasant *Gabbai* [Synagogue sexton] will come and hiss at you telling you to stop!"

Another soldier standing nearby angrily added.

This is unheard of! For a whole year, we hold everything inside, then comes our holy Yom Kippur and we want to cry out and argue with God: Almighty God! How is this possible? How much more torment are Jews to suffer? Are they not already lying pitifully on their faces? Is this also not allowed to us! I have never heard or want to hear about this!

He continued, "With us, in our 'Great Synagogue,' Yom

Kippur is received in fear! A terror! A real Day of Judgment;
we sing *Kol Nidrei*, we hum together the prayer, *unetaneh tokef*
– the earth trembles! "What happens, what we see in our Shul
[Synagogue] is a real Yom Kippur? Here it is different."

The closer the prayers came to the end, the more frequently
soldiers cried out tearful words and deep sighs, while the *gabbaim* [synagogue administrators] would immediately shout:
"Shss!" quieting down the crowd.

Suddenly, near the end of prayers, a tearful voice from a
single Jewish soldier was heard. With a deep broken heart, with
eyes and hands uplifted, he cried aloud: "*Gevalt*, G-d! Almighty
G-d! Have mercy upon your poor people!" His words had a
powerful impact on all the members of the congregation. They
have all been affected by the horrors of the war. The *gabbaim*
forgot to silence people, all present bowed their heads and tears
appeared in every one's eyes.[1]

---

1. Jacob Wygodski, *In Gehinnom: Zichronos fun di Daitcha Tfusos B'shaa der Velt
Milchomo*, Hoiftarkoif Farlang fun B. Kleskin, Vilna, 1927, pp. 94–96

Chapter 6

Fundraising

The following report was one of many published for American Jewry and Jewish communities around the world.

The May 22, 1916 headline stated, "700,000 Jews in Need on East War Front."

The article cited statistics from the German Hebrew Relief Organization.

> Of the normal total of about 2,450,000 Jews in Poland, Lithuania, and Courland, 1,770,000 remain, and of this number about 700,000 in continuous and urgent want. About 455,000 of these are in Poland, and 50,000 of this number are persons who are without homes and are in particularly distressful circumstances. The number of the needy is increasing from month to month. Opportunities to earn money are few and thousands who are still living on their savings will, sooner or later, find these exhausted and become dependent on charity.[2]

American Jewry was confronted with the responsibility of raising funds for their brethren in Europe. At the time of the outbreak of war, there was no infrastructure to raise funds for Jews overseas. A decade had passed since the destructive Kishinev pogroms wreaked havoc, which mobilized American Jewry to political action and fundraising on behalf of the thousands who were left homeless.

Not only were American Jews the greatest source of wealth, but

---

2. *American Jewish Chronicle*, May 22, 1916, p. 85

as a neutral nation until April, 1917, they could better navigate the logistical details of bringing needed supplies through all sides. Media campaigns for support were direct and powerful, commensurate to the need. In Great Britain, The Central Relief Committee issued a public appeal, "A cry of frenzied despair comes from those countries." A plea followed, "GIVE US SOMETHING THAT WE DO NOT DIE." The last line read, "THAT CRY MUST BE ANSWERED."[3]

Fundraising in the United States involved a network of organizations.

On October 4, 1914, the Central Committee for the Relief of Jews (CRC) was formed under the auspices of the Union of Orthodox Jewish Congregations, with Leon Kamicky, editor of the Yiddish daily, *Yiddishe Tageblatt*, as chairman. By July, 1917, it had raised 1.5 million dollars.[4]

On October 24, 1914, the American Jewish Relief Committee (AJRC) was formed by philanthropists and American Jewish leaders, Jacob Schiff, Louis Marshall and Felix Warburg. Six weeks later, on November 27, 1914, it combined with the Orthodox Jewish "Peoples' Relief Committee" to form the American Joint Distribution Committee with Warburg as the chairman.[5]

Jewish labor groups founded the Jewish People's Relief Committee in August, 1915, with socialist congressman, Meyer London, as chairman. By July, 1917, it collected $800,000 and was also affiliated with the J.D.C.[6]

Funds also arrived from B'nai B'rith, *landsmenschaften* (Jewish immigrant societies) and many by individuals unaffiliated with the aforementioned organizations.

Out of concern that some Orthodox groups were not receiving their share of the funds, the rabbinical luminary, Rabbi Chaim Ozer Grodzinski, urged America Orthodox rabbinic leader, Rabbi Eliezer Silver to form another organization, Ezras Torah.

---

3. *LJC*, September 10, 1915, p. 11
4. Morris U. Schappes, *Jewish Life*, "World War One and the Jewish Masses," p. 17
5. Ibid.
6. Ibid.

Relief committee representatives for Eastern European Jewry, Dr. Boris Borgen and Max Senior sent the following cablegram to the American banker, Max Warburg, also chairman of the Joint Distribution Committee, "Official permission was received for distribution throughout Poland and Lithuania apportioning the balance of $300,000 today. For G-D's sake, raise all the money you can. Conditions indescribable. One million people perishing from hunger and cold."[7]

Aid began at the beginning of the war. On August 31, 1914, the American ambassador to Turkey, Henry Morgenthau sent a cable to a leading Jewish philanthropist Jacob Schiff requesting aid for the Jewish community of Palestine. Schiff along with Louis Marshall of the American Jewish Committee immediately raised funds and sent 50,000 dollars in gold on the USS North Carolina which reached the port of Jaffa on October 6.[8]

Supreme Court Justice Louis Brandeis, who was chairman of the New England Committee and addressed several mass meetings for support, stated, "Let every man, woman, and child make a sacrifice, one that hurts for the relief of the unfortunate Jews in the war zone . . . for the sake of humanity." Campaigns spread to other US cities as well.[9]

The first major New York fundraiser was held in Carnegie Hall on December 21, 1915. Three thousand New Yorkers filled the theater, where the agenda was to drum up support in a massive public appeal. After an impassioned two hour address by influential New York Rabbi Judah Magnes, describing the tragedies in Eastern Europe, weeping in the audience was audible. Donations were eagerly offered. One man approached the podium and emptied his pockets depositing some bills and silver into trays. As he walked away, he opened his last pocket and returned to the stage to deposit its contents. Others then rushed forward to give. Women removed their jewelry and deposited them into trays.[10]

---

7. *American Jewish Chronicle*, November 30, 2017, p. 170

8. www.ajcarchives.org/AJC_DTA/Files/F-12.PDF

9. *The Boston Sunday Globe*, March 7, 1915, p. 12

10. *New York Times*, December 22, 1915

However, the campaign fell short of the millions of dollars that were needed. The event collected $700,000.[11] The campaign continued and intensified. Weeks later at the urging of the United States Senate, with the assistance of JDC supporter US Senator James Reed of Missouri, President Woodrow Wilson proclaimed January 27, 1916 as Jewish War Sufferers Relief Day. That year $4,750,000 dollars were reportedly raised.[12]

The famous Cantor Josef (Yossele) Rosenblatt was also part of the effort. He toured the country for extended periods and performed at concerts raising tens of thousands of dollars for the Central Relief Committee.[13]

On November 22, 1917, President Woodrow Wilson sent a letter to Jewish American businessman and philanthropist Jacob Schiff, in support of the campaign, "The American public irrespective of race or creed, should respond liberally to the call for help from stricken Europe. And I feel confident that the needs of the Jewish people in the war zones will find a ready response from their coreligionists in this country." The letter concluded with the words, "assuring you and your associates of my warm support of what you have in mind to accomplish, believe me."[14]

During the campaign which lasted throughout the duration of the war, New Yorker and former US Ambassador to Turkey, Henry Morgenthau, authored a column "A Test for New York Jewry," which was a plea for support "Seldom has a group of people been called upon to stand such a unique moral test."[15]

American Jewish philanthropist, Julius Rosenwald made a one million dollar gift on condition that the pledge was matched by the Relief Committee.[16]

The Joint Distribution Committee channeled funds to the appropriate agencies in Europe, which purchased food, clothing, and medical aid. The Austrian Allianz operated in the Austrian area

11. *New York Times*, December 22
12. Ibid.
13. *America Jewish Chronicle*, March 22, 1918, p. 540
14. *American Jewish Chronicle*, December 17, 1917, p. 170
15. *American Jewish Chronicle*, November 30, 1917, p. 85
16. Oscar Handlin, *A Continuing Task*, p. 27

through offices in Budapest, Lemberg, and Crakow. The Hilfsverein, which was composed of assimilated German Jews, operated in areas under German occupation. On October 2, 1914 the Relief of War Sufferers, (EKOPO), was organized in St. Petersburg, Russia and was supported mostly by Jewish communities in the west. EKOPO groups operated within close proximity to the suffering and were very effective in delivering aid to sufferers.

The KFOD Komitee fur den Osten (Committee for the Jews of the East) was founded by a group of German Zionists led by Max Bodenheimer, on August 17, 1914.

The Joint Distribution Committee which encompassed American Jewish aid groups is alleged to have distributed fifteen million dollars to Jews in need during the war.[17]

Great Britain

An article on the cover of *The Jewish World* journal in London, entitled, "Think of the Poor Afflicted Jews in the Eastern War Zone: Helpless, Homeless, Starving: Relief is Urgently Needed" included an address near the bottom of the page which directed where donations should be sent.[18]

The headline of the January 26, 1916, edition of the *London Jewish Chronicle* contained just three words, "Ruin Starvation Death." The opening editorial on page two stated, "Caught and crushed-in the maelstrom of two opposing armies in the terrible European struggle, the horror, the desperation of their position is unrealizable. . . . Suffice it to say that a huge community has been stricken ruthlessly with ruin, starvation, and death."[19]

Aid to Refugees

The great sage, the Chafetz Chaim, exhorted his fellow Jews to give as generously as possible in housing refugees and providing for them in a manner that allows them as much dignity as possible.

---

17. Handlin, *A Continuing Task*, p. 31
18. *The Jewish World*, March 1, 1916, p. 1
19. *LJC*, January 26, 1917, p. 1–2

Speaking to their hearts, he aroused them to have compassion on their brethren and come swiftly to their aid. He cautioned the people of Smilovitz not to violate the Torah's commandment, *Do not stand idly by the blood of your neighbor (Vayikra* 19:16). He issued a public plea to the rescue of downtrodden Jews. How can we simply observe the evil that is befalling our people?

How can we merely listen impassively to the tribulation of their souls as they beseech us for help?[20]

---

20. Rabbi Moses M. Yoshor, *The Chafetz Chaim: The Life and Works of Rabbi Yisrael Meir Kagan of Radin*, Mesorah Publications, Brooklyn, N.Y., 1994, p. 380

Chapter 7

Letters from German Soldiers at the Front

T he first edition of *War Letters of Fallen German Jews* was published in 1935, while Germany was under the grip of Nazi tyranny and the infamous anti-Semitic Nuremburg Laws were enacted. The purpose of the book was to debunk the charge amid the deluge of anti-Jewish propaganda leveled by the Nazis that the Jews were cowardly and disloyal to Germany during the First World War. The book contained letters from German Jewish soldiers expressing their loyalty and readiness to sacrifice for Germany. The letters, many of which were from 1914, when patriotism was at its highest, are passionate and the descriptions of the fighting reveal the brutal nature of warfare and the intensity of the fighting. Most of the letters published were from soldiers who fell during the war. Some were "parting" letters in event of their deaths. The letters also depict the difficulties faced by the troops in the field and the ferocity of the fighting.

In 1935, the names of Germany's fallen Jews were removed from monuments by the Nazis. This volume was also meant to keep their memories alive.

A Tribute to the Memory of Lieutenant Julius Holz

Lieutenant Infantry Regiment
Profession: bank employee
Born July 5, 1894 in Berlin
Fell June 15, 1918 in Courcelles

December 7, 1916

Dear Father,
As long as my duty keeps me here, I will do what I can to honor
my family as a good German of Jewish faith, I promise you that
on your birthday. I didn't make it quiet by your birthday, but I
am hoping to meet you very soon as a Prussian officer.[21]

Telegram December 11, 1916 (father's birthday)

Promotion to officer by highest cabinet order

April 20, 1917

To the mother,
I am writing this letter only to you because you understand me.
I am not writing this to boast, and not to show you that I did
my duty as a German and officer as best as I could. Because you
who only know of doing your duty, it is self-evident, that I, your
son, do my duty, especially in these difficult days . . .

There was tension between me and Sch. (another officer).
I didn't give in and he was pretty nervous from all the heavy
firings. I haven't slept in three days, because I expected an attack
at any moment. The fourth night he wanted to stay awake,
and told me to rest. I didn't want to and we fought. I was right
because the attack came in the morning, and everything else was
forgotten then – on that day the French took our front trenches,
but we got them back. In the morning the French attacked after
a crazy artillery bombardment. . . . I lost most of my men that

---

21. Franz Josef Strauss, *Kreigsbriefe Gefallener Deutscher Juden, Mit einem Geleit-
wort*, Seewald Verlag, Germany, 1961, p.15

morning, and my entire gun-operating unit, so that I had to fire the weapon myself. I got the order for the whole front line. The French attacked another three times; I threw them back three times, once even though they were already half in my back. And then we got the order to retreat. It was very hard, but we had to, because my people were finished; I only had twelve men left, and I barely could run myself, because I had a splinter in my knee from this morning.

We started our retreat and took with us as booty of a French gun and two quick charging guns. My commander praised me until I blushed, and told me how my wounded men raved about me. I take that as a reward for my self-evident behavior. I am happy that my men know how I was with them in these difficult hours, and that's what you should know my dear mother.[22]

As the war broke out: A Tribute to the Memory of Josef Elkan

Sergeant, 225 Private Infantry Regiment, EKII
Profession: businessman
Born October 24, 1894 in Amberg
Fell August 10, 1918 from wounds

Frankfurt/Main, August 2, 1914

Dear Siegfried!
It is hard for us; we are going through a hard time. Hope you feel better soon and can come back home with G-d's help! I will be assigned patriotic duties, and what counts then is courage, confidence and belief in G-d. The fateful hour has arrived, and who wouldn't give his life for his beloved German mother country? It is a serious time, but with courage and confidence it will come to pass. If we won't see each other again, it was beautiful to die for the mother country.

With brotherly love and kisses,
Your brother Josef [23]

---

22. Ibid. pp. 15–16
23. Ibid. p. 35

A Tribute to the Memory of Berthold Elsaß

Lieutenant of the Reserve
Defense-Infantry Regiment 120
Born August 3, 1885 in Ludwigsburg
Fell May 24, 1916. Despite receiving severe wounds, he continued to serve.

A Letter to a Friend

. . . the war brought me much hardship . . . On August 11 we went to battle with the Reserve Infantry regt. 121 by Hochwald, on August 18 I got my baptism of fire. I will never forget that evening, incapable of thinking, demoralized. On the 19th we attacked Hochfeld which was 1100 meter high, on August 20, Brennstal. There were house battles in Belmont. It went on day and night . . . On the 24th I participated in the attack on the Donon. Here fate caught up with me and I was shot in my hip . . . in the beginning of October I was back with the regiment. I participated in heavy battles against the English and the French. In the night of November 6 we launched three night strikes. A grenade exploded right in front of me, and I lost consciousness. I also had a bad concussion. I was sent to Hagen, were I was lying for months. It wasn't looking good. I was operated three times. First the splint was removed from my head, then another bone. After the third operation the fever and infection got better. My arm and shoulder healed well. The dent in my head gave me trouble and I couldn't wear a helmet. I reported as a volunteer to battle and that's how I came to Defense-Infantry regiment 120 of Bayer III, army corps . . . I am the only Jewish officer in my regiment . . . That's how I went through the war and I feel fine despite the 4 holes in my body . . . We both wouldn't have dreamed that we have to be part of such a murderous war, but hopefully we Jews will be able to finally get equal rights in every way with this war.[24]

---

24. Ibid. p. 36

Memories of Shabbat at home on the eve of battle:
A Tribute to the Memory of Martin Feist

Infantry Regiment 81
Born November 5, 1891 in Frankfurt
Fell November 7, 1915 in France

In the dugout by Andochy, 11/2/14. . . . I want to continue my report from yesterday. The night from Thursday to Friday was quiet. Friday brought us some repose, and exhausted from the exertions, we rested tired in the ditches. Sabbath started, and again we repeated quietly to one another: "Pack the knapsacks, be combat-ready, guns ready." A chill went over me, when I commanded: "tonight attack."

I leaned against the ditch bent over to the front, where we expected the enemy to come from. The full moon helped us to scan the hilly territory. I recited the *Maariv* (evening prayer), and then my thoughts went to you my dear ones. I saw you sitting together at the Shabbat table, sanctified and *besimchoh shel mitzvoh*. (With the joy of observing the Sabbath)

I thought of all the friends and family, and especially about the loyal friend, with the warm heart and glowing ideals . . . Far from his hometown a bullet took his far too young life; I had nothing left besides the memories from happy days of the youth we spent together. G-d's decisions are inscrutable. I was reminiscing for hours and stopped at the thought of the horrors that my eyes have seen. You, who stayed home, are so lucky that you were spared to see the horror of the war. . . .

The moon disappeared behind dark clouds. It became quiet and dark around me when to my right a massive rifle fire began. The cannons thundered, machine guns rumbled constantly, the French attack had started. We emerged as the winner in the morning; but it had cost some brave comrades their lives.

Saturday was quiet. I made *Havdalah* (ceremony marking the conclusion of the Shabbat) with old coffee from my bottle, a cigar for *besomim*, and sang *zmirot* (Sabbath songs) to myself. The belief in *Hakadosh Baruch Hu* (G-d) accompanies me from

Shabbat into the week. He will look after me and protect me, and with his help we will see each other healthy again. . . .[25]

A Tribute to the Memory of Arthur Kaufmann

War volunteer
Pioneer Battalion, high school graduate
Born August 8, 1897 in Kehl am Rhein
Fell February 8, 1915 from wounds

December 12, 1914

My dear!
Even though I am far from you, I did not forget that tonight the Chanukah candles are lit, and the memories of how we stood around dear father every year with joyful expectation, as he lit the Chanukah candles with festive singing, kept coming back, together with the tunes of *Maoz Tzur Yeshuassi*. Tonight the candle of joy will not be lit, neither will there be any singing. But, dear parents, just as the Maccabees fought for a holy cause, so do your sons fight for right and equality . . . and, when we come back victors from this battle, then we can light the holy light to thank G-d and join in the old happy song with renewed joy.[26]

A Tribute to the Memory of Gotthold Kronheim

Sub officer, 53rd Regiment
Profession: Pharmacy Apprentice
Born July 24, 1889 in Samotchin
Fell November 19, 1917

Gotthold Kronheim writes below of the anti-Semitism he experienced in the army, while always holding onto the hope of being treated as an equal.
. . . this is the second time I volunteered in the war, even

---

25. Ibid. p. 40–41
26. Ibid. p. 65

though I had experienced affronts and insults of all kinds as a Jew. According to our Kaiser there should not be any more parties, only German people, but so far I only encountered affronts, and recognition was not yet granted to me yet. But I still did my duty for my mother country and I am proud of it, and it makes me forget all the petty and narrow-minded views. As a German Jew, I defended my mother country the best I could. I wish that Germany should come out of the horror of the war as a winner and that it will start judging our actions instead of our faith . . .[27]

A Tribute to the Memory of Herman Samuel

Lieutenant of the Reserve, 21. Bayer
Infantry Regiment, EKII
Born February 24, 1892 in Karbath
Fell November 27, 1914 in storm on Apremont

A posthumous letter

November 27, 1914

My dears! If you get this letter, I sacrificed my life for our mother country. What does the individual mean in these great times in which so many of our best have died! And that's why I hope that you bear my fate the way it becomes to Germans and Jews: composed and devoted to G-d, this is my last wish . . . .[28]

A Tribute to the Memory of Bei Dixmuiden

November 3, 1914

. . . I am writing this letter during an artillery barrage, which didn't reach us, because we are the reserve. Finally, eight long, fearful days our 3rd. battalion was in the front line. It is a miracle that I emerged unwounded from these battles. I don't want to describe to you how a grenade hit in front of me and all

---

27. Ibid. p. 74–75
28. Ibid. pp. 104–105

my comrades feared for my life. I got up from the ashes like a phoenix.[29]

A Tribute to the Memory of Max Strauss

Sub officer 1
Profession: Teacher
Born December 25, 1882 in Hofheim
Fell September 6, 1914 from his wounds

From his legacy

August 6, 1914

I follow the call of the mother country in this serious hour and leave with faith in G-d, the conductor of all fates, to fight the enemy who threatens it. I put my soul into your hands, oh G-d, do with it what you feel is right with your goodness and mercy.

If you decide that I should die for the mother country, I thank you for it, because you do good, "Your name should be praised."[30]

A Tribute to the Memory of Julius Holz

A Mother's Tragic Cry

A young Jewish volunteer, Julius Holz, in a letter to his father on his twentieth birthday, on December 7, 1914, vowed to, "Fight like a man, and as a good German of true Jewish faith and for the greater honor of my family." Holz fell in battle in 1918. Twenty-four years later, on the eve of her deportation to a death camp, his eighty-one year old mother wrote to authorities asking that she be spared considering her son's death in action as attested by the enclosed documents. She received a one line reply: "your application to be released from 'labor service' is refused."[31]

---

29. Ibid. pp. 107–108
30. Ibid. pp. 120–121
31. Elon, *The Pity of it All*, p. 308

Chapter 8

Excerpts and Letters from the Anglo Jewish Press About the Troops

A Passover prayer by a soldier

To keep the Seder in the trenches, or in cantonments, or on the frontier, is, after all, a near approach to the circumstances under which the children of Israel took their unleavened bread on their departure from Egypt. Like our forefathers, we may have, some of us, to eat it in haste, with our loins girded for battle. . . . . May the protection of G-D, whose covering Hand was outstretched over our ancestors on the first great *Lel Shimurim* [The Night of Protection] likewise safeguard tonight, while they recite the Haggadah, both our comrades from the dangers of battle, and our parents and dear ones from the perils of the air.[32]

The following is a description of the death of a German Jewish officer during a pitch battle with British troops.

In the course of a letter from squadron Sergeant Major V. Wrathbone, of the King Edward's Horses, to his brother Mr. M Wrathbone. The former writes,

I was up and down the trenches for twenty-four hours, with one hour's rest. We captured a German officer, Lieut. Max Seller,

---

32. *LJC* June 28, 1918, Quoted from Herbert Loewe, '*Davar B'ito*' (a word in its time) pp. 26–27

of a Bavarian Cavalry Regiment. He and about fifty men were attacking us with hand bombs and the officer was bayonetted on the parapet. I helped to bury him with our own casualties. He was a Jew so I had the services altered by the Chaplain. He was a plucky chap and our fellers could not help expressing admiration at his effort to bomb us.[33]

The following excerpt is about a 16-year-old Jew in the Russian army who was taken prisoner by the Austrians.

On seeing before him a mere boy, the enemy (who happened to be Austrians) thought they could easily get information out of him as to the number and disposition of Russian forces. But the boy would not say a word, and with disgust the Austrians threw him into a barn guarded by a soldier. In the night he escaped, and arrived safely at the Russian headquarters, where he supplied valuable information about the enemy. In the next battle, he so distinguished himself that he was made a corporal on the spot. This is a case without precedent in the Russian army.[34]

The following is one of several stories of soldiers protected by their *tefillin*.

Nathan Loew of a South Hungarian regiment prayed regularly on the battlefield, despite the remarks and taunts of other troops. One morning he moved near the enemy position, and was noticed by the Serbians who opened fire. Others fled, some were wounded. He continued to *daven* [pray] with *tefillin*. As he was removing his *tefillin*, the bugle sounded and an attack was launched. Nathan mounted his horse and defended his position. Only after the attack did he manage to unwind his *tefillin*. A legend arose among fellow troops that the straps were bulletproof

---

33. *The Jewish World*, June 30, 1915, p.20
34. *The Jewish World*, March 10, 1915, p. 10

and other soldiers wanted to confiscate them and cut them to pieces to distribute among themselves.[35]

A Bar Mitzvah and Soldier

A boy named Shmuel Brody who became a Bar Mitzvah last January, left his home in January, changed his named to Jack Hamilton, and gave his age as nineteen. He managed to enlist as a private in the British army. He finally wrote two letters to his parents in May, signing the letters as from "Your fighting son Sam."[36]

Underage

> Probably one of the youngest members of the British Army today is Private Michael Cowen of Burnley, who belongs to the 4th Manchester Regiment. At the outbreak of the war when he was only 14 ½ years of age, he left home, and his mother, who resides in Parliament Street published "missing from home" notices concerning him. She subsequently ascertained that he had enlisted, and was stationed near Hull. He is at present with the Expeditionary Force in France. His mother states: "Of Jewish nationality, he is a fine lad, and we are proud of him. He has set an example that is worthy of note."[37]

In July, 1914, a young Russian Jew studying in Switzerland could not return to Russia so he went to Paris and fought for the French. A month later he was severely wounded. Incapacitated when discharged from the hospital, the French gave him 400 franks and he returned via Sweden and Finland to Russia. He went to Petrograd and was expelled with his fellow Jews, and forced out back into the Pale Settlement.[38]

The Jew, Mordechai Kazap of Kishinev [Russia], who was liable

---

35. *Bnei B'rith News*, December, 1914, p. 6
36. *LJC*, June 4, 1915, p. 22
37. *LJC*, June 18, 1915, p. 20
38. *The Jewish World*, May 5, 1915, p.25

to military service, was sentenced to the usual fine of 300 rubles, because the latter had not presented himself for service. The relatives proved by documents that the alleged "deserter" had been fighting in the British army at the Dardanelles, and had been wounded. But this proof was of no avail. A poor brother of the missing man had to pay 300 rubles [as a fine].[39]

> While aliens [immigrants without British citizenship] might have doubted the war cause, Lance Sergeant Harry Schenthal in a letter to his father, speaks for other native British Jews when he writes,
> It is splendid to see so many of our denomination serving for so good a cause, which is a righteous one. We must remember that in no part of the world is a Jew treated so freely as in England, and it is up to us to do our precious duty to our gracious King and country.[40]

A letter by Private I Levy of the British Army in a letter to his parents describes the ferocity of the fighting. He writes,

> Last Sunday, we had to attack a certain place at the point of the bayonet; but when we got near the Germans, we had nearly all our officers and N.C.O.s (non-commissioned officers) and men killed or wounded; so we had to retire. I, for one could not do so as I was far too advanced, so I had to lie on my stomach all day under heavy shell and maxim fire. It was horrible lying there hearing the wounded groaning and crying for water which we could not give them.[41]

First Experience of Fire

> This was my first experience under fire and it was hot there I can tell you. First of all rifle fire from all directions – there were

---

39. *The American Hebrew*, February 18, 1916, p. 9
40. *LJC*, June 4, 1915, p. 22
41. Ibid. p.21

four wounded and then we had to make a dash to save the guns – and dash we did. The shrapnel from the German guns were bursting all around us. Two of our officers had their horses shot from under them. Gun team horses fell like logs but that never stopped us. My own team managed to hook the gun on the limber; then the trouble started. We stayed under fire for the most terrible description for about three to five minutes. Having sighted the traces we eventually got away with our officer hanging on breaching of the gun. The battery came into action again in a cornfield to cover the retreat of the infantry, but we never stayed there long. The enemy seemed to be everywhere. It was a terrible sight, wounded lay about on our retreat and the ambulance was unable to get near them owing to the German guns firing on the ambulance – a dirty trick of savage warfare.[42]

More from the Anglo Press

"The Jews and the War in Russia" By Princess Catherine Radziwill[43]

I loved my country better than my life and liberty which I was enjoying in America, so I decided to return to Russia and I landed at Arkhangel. I was accepted in the army and lost my arm at the shoulder. I was sent to Courland. I had scarcely reached Riga when the first sight which met my eyes was that of my mother and father and other members of my family at the railway station waiting for a train that was to carry them away to an unknown destination. They had expelled them that same day by order of the military authorities. I want to tell you that I did not regret the loss of my arm so much as that of my dignity as a human being, which I enjoyed while I was in America.[44]

---

42. *LJC*, Letters from The Front, February 19, 1915, pp. 20–21

43. Princess Catherine Radziwill was a Polish aristocrat who was also a noted author.

44. *The Jewish Tribune*, April 1, 1921

Mendel Bigaier

When the Russians marched into Rzeszow, Galitzia, Mendel Bigaier,an American citizen who had come to visit his relatives, was among others suddenly attacked by Cossacks, and robbed of 1,300 Kronen in the presence of the commanding officer. Bigaier said indignantly to the commander; "Sir, you have not soldiers here but robbers!" The commander answered, "You will be hanged within a half hour." He ordered his men to lead the Jew away. Bigaier told him in the last moment, "You will pay dearly for this. I am an American citizen." The Russians made inquiries and learned that Bigaier was really from New York and an American citizen and he was immediately released.[45]

In the Arms of the Enemy

A wounded officer of the Austrian Army, a Jew, was taken prisoner, and the local rabbi of the "enemy" country visited the poor man, sending him comforts and necessaries. After a day or so it was found that an operation was necessary, and the rabbi promised a fatal result. Resting in the rabbi's arms he passed away while the last rights of the dying were administered to him. In accordance with the wish expressed to him by the officer, the rabbi wrote to the dead soldier's father, breaking to him in gentle and considerate language the bad tidings, and telling him that the rabbi was with his son to the last. The rabbi duly received an acknowledgement, warmly thanking him for all he had done, the father expressing his deep obligations. He said he was sure the rabbi had done all he could in the circumstances to assuage the last moments of his son, "but," he added, "the loss is a terrible one to me! Not merely because I lost a dear son, but because to my dying day there will be for me the mortification that my poor boy died in the arms of an enemy."[46]

---

45. *Bnei Brith News*, March, 1915, p.1
46. *LJC*, December 25, 1914, p. 8, quoted from *The Jewish World*

Expelled with Fellow Jews from Petrograd

In July, 1914, a young Russian Jew studying in Switzerland could not return to Russia, so he went to Paris and fought for the French. A month later he was so severely wounded and incapacitated when discharged from the hospital, that the French gave him 400 franks and he returned via Sweden and Finland to Russia. He went to Petrograd and was expelled with his fellow Jews, forced out, back into the Pale Settlement.[47]

In 1916, when the British instituted the mandatory draft there were over twenty-five thousand able bodied young men from Eastern Europe in the Jewish ghettos of East London. Because they were not naturalized citizens they were not subject to service unless they volunteered. The fact that many were not interested since Great Britain was allied with Russia was a source of embarrassment to native British Jews. The following excerpt from the *LJC* is about a Russian born Jew, Private Max Markowitz, who served with distinction.

> On the outbreak of war he joined the army, although not naturalized, while the local authority took the responsibility. A week ago his mother and sister received news that Private Markowitz had been killed in action. Although an alien, he served England as a true patriot, and many letters of sympathy were received by his relatives.[48]

---

47. *The Jewish World*, May 5, 1915, p.25
48. *LJC*, January 7, 1916, p. 13

Chapter 9

Austria

Over two million Jews lived within the Austro-Hungarian Empire at the outbreak of the war. More than 300,000 of them served in the Austro-Hungarian army. Alongside the usual motives of patriotism, there was an additional incentive for the Austro-Hungarian soldier.

Before the war, about 200,000 Jews resided in the Austrian capital of Vienna, out of a population of two million. As with other nations which were westernized, Jews in the larger cities tended to be more assimilated into the larger culture. Despite the varied backgrounds of Jews within the duel empire, they all shared admiration for the Emperor Franz Joseph. The monarch rose to the throne in 1848, and soon began to issue new legislation regarding the Jews. (By 1867, he granted them emancipation.) The Austrian army as well was more tolerant than others. While there were numerous reported incidents of anti-Semitism, there were fewer than in other armies. Bogus charges of disloyalty against Jews so often leveled in other countries were more often disregarded in Austria. However, that was not always the case. An appeal published in the *Israelit* of Frankfurt from Austrian Jews called to their German brethren to assist in combating anti-Semitism within the empire. The reason given for this appeal was that "racial anti-Semitism has been imported from Germany."[49]

There were also many times when the army made painstaking efforts to obtain religious items such as Passover provisions for Jewish soldiers. Army life had varied affects upon the personal lives of

49. *LJC*, April 30, 1915, p.10

Austrian Jewish troops. The more assimilated Jews in service were more exposed to traditional Jewry, while more traditional Jews accustomed to a more insular world came in greater contact with outside influences.

A Hungarian Rabbi at the Front

In 1867 the kingdoms of Hungary and Austria merged, becoming the Constitutional Monarchy otherwise known as the Austro-Hungarian Empire until its fall at the end of World War One.

Rabbi Leopold (Yekutiel Yehudah) Greenwald (1888–1955,) was born in Transylvania and immigrated to the United States in 1924 with his family. For almost thirty years he was the spiritual leader of Congregation Beth Jacob of Columbus Ohio.[50]

Rabbi Greenwald served as a chaplain in the Hungarian army. Although he was exempt from army service on account of his status as a rabbi, he nonetheless volunteered out of patriotism and a sense of appreciation to the Austro-Hungarian Emperor Franz Joseph.[51] He enlisted and served as a common soldier and was wounded by a bayonet receiving a scar below his eye. He also contracted malaria and when released from the hospital, became a telegrapher.[52]

Rabbi Greenwald authored many volumes including *Sefer Zichronot*, (Book of Remembrances) which details his experiences during the war. Rabbi Greenwald wrote at some length of his disappointment with the army as a result of his experiences.

Many Austrian Jews in the military claimed to have not experienced much anti-Semitism; however, that was not the experience of Rabbi Greenwald. From the moment of induction, he claimed to have encountered anti-Semitism. He was often beaten and abused by his commanders, who hurled anti-Semitic epitaphs at him. He, noted, "Yesterday, I was an honored member of my community, to-

---

50. Rabbi Greenwald participated in the Rabbi's march on behalf of European Jewry in Washington D.C., on October 6, 1943

51. *Sefer Zichronot*, Yekutial Yehudah Greenwald, Budapest, Published by Katzberg Brothers, 1922, p. 7

52. Based upon conversations with the author's son, Mr. Jack Greenwald of Denver Colorado.

day, I am hated and despised."[53] Rabbi Greenwald wrote that Jews in the army were singled out for abuse, and that the anti-Semitism was rife in the army.[54] Nonetheless, despite all, he sought to remain loyal, encouraging his fellow Jewish soldiers to remain focused on achieving victory for their country.[55] After a particular victory, he celebrated, explaining to an officer that he too belongs to Hungary, and it was also his victory. He also explained that he was ready to die for Hungary. The response by the officer was that being a Jew, he was not part of the nation. This prompted Rabbi Greenwald to pose the rhetorical question, "Why are we fighting?"[56] as if to say; why should a Jew fight for an army that does not really acknowledge his citizenship on account of his being a Jew? Yet, he still advised fellow Jewish soldiers not to despair and lose hope."[57] On Yom Kippur of that year, Rabbi Greenwald was asked to address fellow troops at services where he conveyed a somber message, stating, "We were mistaken, my friends, mistaken!" He continued, "We thought that common sense would protect us, we were sure that evil would not descend upon us. Rather, fellow troops and officers hate us and seek to harm us. . . . ."[58] However, according to the rabbi, the situation improved for the Jewish members of his unit with a change in command and that the sense of camaraderie with fellow troops also eventually improved as a result.[59] Despite all, he still spoke of his adoration for Hungary.[60]

Dr. Joseph Tenenbaum was a surgeon and author who later became a Zionist leader. In 1919, he was a member of the Jewish delegation at the post war Paris peace conference. During the war, he served as a physician for the Austrian army, and wrote of his experiences in

---

53. Sefer Zichronot, Yekutial Yehudah Greenwald, Budapest, Published by Katzberg Brothers, 1922, p. 11
54. Ibid. p. 18
55. Ibid. p. 41
56. Ibid. p. 45
57. Ibid. p. 46
58. Ibid. p. 51
59. Ibid. p. 71
60. Ibid. p. 87

his book *'in Fir'* ("Under Fire.") Following, are three of his stories as a doctor on the battle field in the former Austro-Hungarian army.

While searching for the wounded from battle, Dr. Tenenbaum saw a boy on the battle field, and instructed his assistants to carry the boy to the hospital. Dr. Tenenbaum asked him his name and the boy replied, "Heshcele." Herschele asked him for a drink, and then a hat so he could recite the blessing. He was given a soldiers cap. Tanenbaum asked him about the whereabouts of his father, he replied that he never knew him. What about his mother? He claimed he remembered her in a dream. He stated that his grandmother just passed away and had requested that he say *Kaddish* (prayer for the deceased). But where, he asked, could he say *Kaddish*? For three days, he was alone with no shelter and he just wept. When he heard shooting and noticed that the Russians were in retreat, he followed them. While running, he hurried into a *Beit HaMidrash* (Jewish House of learning). He was shot in the foot.

While in the hospital, Herschele soon became a friend of the soldiers. One soldier in the regiment taught him to recite the *Kaddish*, and as he finished pronouncing the words, all the soldiers, Jews and Gentiles alike, responded *Amen* – everyone was inspired by the boy. Heschele was a helping hand to the soldiers, going into towns to find troops and bringing them provisions. He also brought bottles of water to soldiers in the field during battles. It was a dangerous task which he performed for over six months.

One day during a fierce skirmish, the Austrians managed to retake a field. Among the mortally wounded lay Herschele. He was found grasping a bottle of water in his hand. All the soldiers felt a deep sense of sympathy for the boy who lay mortally wounded.[61]

1. For the Kaiser

Another experience that Dr. Tenenbaum shares describes an elderly Jew, loyal to the Kaiser. As the Austrians were liberating towns in Galitzia from Russian control, in one very quiet village, many soldiers

---

61. Joseph Tenenbaum, *In Fire*, Max Meizel and Company, New York, 1926, p. 41

gathered around an elderly man with a *shtriemel* (Hasidic hat for the Sabbath and festivals) and *bekishe* (Hasidic coat). When he saw the Austrian soldiers, he began dancing and singing. He then proceeded to bless the king and the queen. The soldiers were entertained by his display of patriotism. However, when some soldiers began to harass the Jew, a command was shouted out that everyone should leave him alone. He soon ended his performance and returned to his home. When he was asked the reason for his behavior, he responded, telling the tragic story of his family and their suffering at the hands of the Russians. His wife was killed. Two of his children died of typhus, and he was left with one surviving daughter. He watched over her, but when the Russians arrived, they violated her and took her away. Then he was all alone. "I did not suffer in vain," He proclaims, "I had the joy of fasting and praying for the victory of the Kaiser." He asked if the Emperor Franz Joseph would take St. Petersburg from the Russians. When he was then informed that the emperor had recently passed away, his demeanor suddenly changed, he collapsed to the floor weeping. The unit returned to the front, and the Russians soon retook the town. However, a week later, the Austrians returned. Dr. Tenenbaum went to inquire about the elderly man. He was informed that when the Russians entered, they saw a home with a man wearing a *tallis* (prayer shawl) through the window, and the Austrian flag hanging outside. They entered the house and beat him to death. The Austrian army gave him a soldier's funeral. On his tombstone, the inscription stated, here lies Avraham the Austrian patriot.[62]

2. A Post Armistice Get Together and Dreams of Zion

The fighting in the East ended on March 3, 1918, with the Brest-Litovsk Treaty signed between Russia and Germany. One day Tenenbaum received an invitation from a Russian physician in the army named Hoft to join them for celebrations on their grounds. He accepted the offer despite the prohibition and attended the celebration accompanied by two lieutenants. To reach the party, he had to trek

---

62. Ibid. p. 19

through back roads and heavy snow.[63] On the way, the remnants of battles – signs of the destruction – were evident. They finally reached their destination, which was a scene of celebration. Tenenbaum entered a home partially destroyed by artillery. Guests had already arrived. He was approached by many people and embraced. He was soon introduced to Dr. Hoft, and a group of doctors.[64] Drinking and conversation ensued. Many Russian officers at the party spoke about Russian leaders and the Revolution that was taking place. Most expressed opposition to the revolution. Some called for the death of the leader of the provisional government, Alexander Kerensky. As they were vigorously engaged in debate, the two doctors Tenenbaum had first met were conversing in Yiddish. Tenenbaum joined their conversation. One of the Russian doctors, while relating his experiences at the battle front, stated that a year ago he had met a Jewish soldier lamenting as to why the Russian military was engaged in Galitzia. The soldier spoke of the slaughter of Jews by the Cossacks. Tenenbaum then told the Russian doctors about the crimes against the Jews that the Cossacks had committed in Galitzia. Together, they shared the misery of their people's suffering under Russian occupation. Their conversations soon led to talks about Palestine. They expressed their support for the aims of Zionism and declared, "It is worth sacrificing for Palestine." After the merriment and dancing, Russian national songs were sung. There, the three doctors began singing the Zionist national anthem, Hatikvah, loud enough for the Russians to hear. The three Jews, one from an opposing side, were far from Palestine but they were united in their dreams.[65]

---

63. Ibid. p. 134
64. Ibid. p. 136
65. Ibid. pp.140–142

Chapter 10

The Russian Revolution

The Russian Revolution of March, 1917 was the first stage – the earlier revolution which lead to the Bolshevik Revolution later that year. Rioters and strikers in the capital city of St. Petersburg, and other locations refused to desist in their efforts to cause chaos. At the time, there was mutiny in the army as regiments of the Czar's army defected. Czar Nicholas II, who was losing control of his empire, abdicated the throne.

Most of the world which follows the Gregorian calendar refers to this event as the March Revolution since it took place on March 8. To the Russians who once followed the Julian calendar which places the day at February 23, it was the February Revolution.

War, hunger and poverty had fueled the rage. The immense damage and destruction to Russia caused by its involvement in the First World War contributed significantly to the fall of the Czar. Approximately two million soldiers were reported dead, many more were seriously wounded, the economy was in shambles and unemployment was running rampant.

A new provisional government was established. At the helm was the socialist democrat Alexander Kerensky who became the Minister of Justice. At the same time, Kerensky also became the vice-chairman of the Petrograd (St. Petersburg) Soviet revolutionary council. These posts made him the most important leader in the revolution. The expectation was that the government would exercise a more tolerant rule than its predecessors.

Within the Jewish community, many saw a departure in the change of leadership from the despotism and anti-Semitism of the Czar.

Kerensky had sympathized with the plight of the Jews under the Czarist regime. He was one of the sponsors of a resolution by the Saint Petersburg bar condemning the 1913 trial of Mendel Beilis, falsely accused of ritual murder, as a "slanderous attack upon the Jewish People." He himself had personally investigated and refuted the highly publicized bogus charges of treason leveled against the Jews in Kuzhi in April, 1915.[66]

Just ten days after the abdication of the Czar, the new provisional government had officially granted freedom to the long beleaguered Jewish community of Russia. These freedoms included residing where they pleased, participating in all educational advantages, voting and owning property.

Some in the Jewish community in Russia and around the world responded enthusiastically. The following is just a sample of the outpouring of enthusiasm.

With unbridled enthusiasm, Jewish author and activist Shmarya Levin asked, "Will the Jews for the first time in our history, become free, not as dismembered individuals, but as a national minority?"[67]

In the words of Rabbi Enelow of Temple Emanuel of New York,

> There has never been a more complete, nor a more wonderful transformation than that wrought by the Russian Revolution in the condition of the Jew. One of the first consequences of the Revolution was the abolition of Jewish disabilities, the specific abrogation of all Jewish restrictions, the repudiation of all laws and regulations against them that countries had accumulated – the instant recognition of the Jew.[68]

In the journal, the *American Hebrew*, one opinion piece proclaimed, "The first French Revolution declared the Jews to be human beings,

---

66. 301. See page 33 regarding the Kuzhi allegations.

67. Dr. Shemarya Levin, *The Russian Revolution*, The Maccabaean, April, 1917, p. 2–9

68. Rabbi H.G. Enelow D.D., *The Allied Counties and the Jews, a Series of Addresses*, Temple Emanuel, New York, 1918, p. 41

the last Russian Revolution proclaimed the Jews to be free citizens, a nation of freemen."[69]

An editorial in the same journal one week later opined, "With the absolute equality of Jews in Russia, the bloodiest chapter in Jewish history then comes to an end."[70]

One letter to the editor of the *American Hebrew* on March 23, 1917, proposed that "March 15, the day of the abdication of the Czar be turned into a Jewish holiday." Adding, "Everyone will admit that that day will be forever the greatest day of joy in the Jewish calendar."[71]

An editorial in *the London Jewish Chronicle* stated that, "There are firm hopes that the dark days of oppression never return. With our great friend Mr. Kerensky as the moving spirit of the new government and Mr. Zarudni [the defender of Mendel Beilis who faced a blood libel accusation in 1913] as his assistant at the Ministry of Justice, the Russian Jews cannot only breathe freely, but they can also, with a clear mind, attend to their national problems of the hour."[72]

The results would turn out to be far different than the hopes. The provisional government was very young and vulnerable. Revolutionary Marxist leader of the Bolshevik Party, Vladimir Lenin, who returned from exile in Switzerland with the assistance of Germany, which sought his leadership over Russia, helped foment revolution to topple the Kerensky government. In order to maintain Western alliances, Kerensky, who had become Minister of War in May, 1917, had kept Russia in the war and launched another attack against Austria-Hungary into the region of Galicia, the Second Brusilov Offensive, which turned out to be a very costly failure. Lenin who opposed the war had promised the suffering Russian people "Land, Bread, and Peace," earning him sufficient support from local Soviet revolutionary councils, to mount a partial takeover of parts of the Russian Empire, and realize much of his plans in November, 1917. By 1921, the rest of the empire would be under Soviet control.

---

69. M. Katz, The *American Hebrew*, March 23, 1917, p. 606
70. The *American Hebrew*, March 26, 1917, p. 647
71. Isidor Singer, *American Hebrew*, March 23, 1917, p. 611
72. *LJC*, April 27, 1917, p. 10

The Bolshevik Revolution would cause immeasurable suffering. While the Russian Revolution of 1917 did not initially incur substantial losses, decades of horrors under Soviet dictatorships followed. Millions perished from persecution, terror, and in gulags.

The Bolshevik Revolution would also produce dangerous and destructive forms of anti-Semitism as the Jewish communist group, the Yevsekztia, spied on and betrayed fellow Jews who maintained Jewish observances despite the religious bans that were imposed. Zionists, as well, were persecuted.

Although such groups represented a very small minority of the Jews, the damage they would cause was considerable.

Chapter 11

The Yanks Are Coming

On June 26, 1917, just over two months after America's entry into the war, American troops began to arrive in France. On October 21, the first Americans were in combat. For the next year, two million American troops fighting alongside the Entente would change the course of the war. Four million were drafted and fifty-thousand would make the ultimate sacrifice.

Since the Russian Revolution and the subsequent Brest-Litovsk Treaty on March 3, 1918, between Russia and Germany, Russia's involvement in the war was over leaving just the Western Front in Europe as the main European theatre. America's entry prevented the continuation of the stalemate which could have tilted towards the Central Powers due to the increased concentration of German forces there.

By July, 1918, over one million U.S. troops were in France. Of the approximately 225,000 Jews who served in the US armed forces, 1,100 were cited for valor. Three soldiers received the Congressional Medal of Honor.

A few of those heroes are mentioned here.

On October 4, 1918, Sergeant Benjamin Kaufman of the 308th Infantry was separated from his platoon. With his right arm shattered by a bullet, Kaufman advanced upon the German line throwing grenades with his left hand while charging with an empty pistol. He captured the machine gun crew and returned with the pistol and a prisoner.[73]

---

73. Captain Sydney G. Gumpertz, *The Jewish Legion of Valor*, Published by Syd-

William Sawelson of the 312th Infantry on October 28, 1918, heard a wounded soldier nearby calling for water. He crawled through heavy enemy fire and gave from his own canteen. While returning to the wounded man with more provisions he was struck by a machine gun bullet and killed. The Medal of Honor on his behalf was presented to his father.[74]

The companies of "The Lost Battalion" of the 77th Division were given that title due to their isolation by German forces from other units. They were made up mostly of immigrants from the Lower East Side of Manhattan: forty percent of the division was Jewish. Consisting of about 554 men, during the Argonne Campaign, in October, 1918, they unknowingly advanced with no flank support. Despite being surrounded, they held their ground, allowing for the arrival of reinforcements. Of the Battalion, 197 were killed, about 150 were missing or taken prisoner while the remaining 194 were rescued.

Among the heroes of the 77th was Private Jack Herschkowitz who was awarded the Distinguished Service Cross. Herschkowitz, along with another soldier, was attacked by a small party of Germans, managing to kill one before they were driven off. When night arrived the two unknowingly crawled into the middle of a German camp. Upon being discovered they fled and Herschkowitz intentionally drew the fire towards himself in order to protect the officer. The next morning, he managed to deliver the intended message as per his mission.[75]

Private Abraham Krotoshinsky also of the 77th Battalion alongside was awarded the Congressional Medal of Honor. At great peril, while other messengers on the same mission were shot down, he successfully passed a message which saved the remnants of the beleaguered battalion (by informing the US army of their situation and position). In his own words,

I got my orders and started. It was five o'clock in the morning

---

ney G. Gumpertz, New York, 1941, p. 195
   74. Ibid. p. 193
   75. MilitaryTimes.Com/Citations

on October 7th. I had to run about thirty feet in plain view of the Germans before I got into the forest. They saw me when I got up and fired everything they had at me. I could feel the bullets whistle around me but I didn't get hit once. I guess it wasn't *"bashert"* that I should get killed by the Germans. Then I had to crawl right through their lines. They were looking for me everywhere. I just moved along on my stomach, in the direction I was told, keeping my eyes open for them. The brush was six feet high and often that saved me. Once a squadron of Germans passed right by my hiding place jabbing their bayonets into the thicket and swearing like the devil. One big fellow nearly stepped on my hand. He looked right into my eye. I thought I was finished at the time. But he never saw me."[76]

A senior Chaplin of the 77th Division, Rabbi Elkan Voorsanger, was also known as the fighting rabbi of World War One. When the troops left the trenches to attack the Germans, Rabbi Voorsanger also went with them and he was highly decorated. Among his awards was the Purple Heart. In his words, "The Jewish men in this division were good soldiers, brave, fearless, and resourceful. They fought, knew how to fight and were glad to do it."[77]

The heroism of the 77th made significant contributions to the American victory and remains legendary in the annals of US military history.

---

76. Abraham Krotoshinsky, *The Jewish Criterion*, "His Own Story," September 12, 1919, p.9

77. Online archives of the JDC, WWI, and Jewish Telegraphic Agency, May 6, 1963, obituary.

Chapter 12

Zion

National rehabilitation is due the Jewish people.[78]

For almost all of the prior four-hundred years, the Ottoman Turks controlled the Land of Israel. In order to save their fledgling empire, the official Turkish entry into the war on October 28, 1914 signaled bad tidings for all the inhabitants of the land, especially for the Jewish community, which would face a wave of persecution. When the war broke out there were between 90,000 and 95,000 Jews living in Palestine, over 50,000 of whom made their homes in Jerusalem. The Jewish community was made up of the Old Yishuv, whose ancestors, over the centuries, relocated to Palestine with the purpose of residing within the land. They were mostly poor and subsisted upon *Chalukah* (Hebrew word for distribution), an organized collection and distribution of charity funds from Jewish communities abroad. There was also the New Yishuv, comprised of Zionists, mostly younger, who made their way to the land within the most recent decades with the purpose of developing the land and building a Jewish state.

Even before their official entry into the war, the Turks, who had already committed themselves to the side of the Central Powers were already pressing Muslim, Christian, and Jewish men in Palestine into military service. They also had already begun to requisition supplies. Civilians were forced to contribute to the Ottoman war cause. They requisitioned horses and carts, and opened stores of grain, cut down

---

78. *The Maccabaean*, October, 1917, p. 362

trees, handed over arms, and received soldiers billeted to them. After the declaration of war, such activities would significantly increase.

Some Zionists within the land did initially greet the Ottoman declaration of war enthusiastically. They had placed their hopes in the central powers and Turkey to facilitate a Jewish state, but the Turks would show no such interest. These Jews could have potentially been allies to the Turks. Many had considered allegiance to the Ottomans with the hope that Palestine's Jews would be permitted to establish a Jewish militia to protect their communities. Instead, they were suspected by the Turks of allying with the French and British in hopes of gaining their support for Jewish statehood.

Another reason many Zionists initially supported the Turks was the fear that allying with the British and the Entente would elicit severe retribution from the Turks. The risk of supporting the Entente for many was considered too great. There was also a widely held expectation that the Central Powers would be victorious so hopes were placed in Turkey. Some Jews enlisted to fight for the Ottoman Empire. The future first Israeli Prime Minister, David Ben Gurion, and the future second president of Israel, Yitzchak ben Tzvi expressed interest in joining with the Turks.[79] The two set up a "Yishuv Ottomization Committee," with the expressed purpose of raising a Jewish fighting force aligned with the Turks. In addition, a document dated April 6, 1915, reports on a proposal "made at one time by an engineer Loewy for the protection of Jewish colonization by the formation of a Turkish aligned militia."[80] Eliezer ben Yehudah who was responsible for reviving Hebrew into a modern spoken language, endorsed the idea of Jews becoming Ottoman subjects. So did Meir Dizingoff, future mayor of Tel Aviv, and other leaders in the Yishuv.[81]

Some local Jews showed support for the Ottoman Turks out of loyalty. At a local parade in support of the empire, one of the draftees,

---

79. Ben Gurion and Ben Tzvi would soon be expelled from Palestine by Djemal Pasha.

80. *Herzl Year Book*, Volume 7, Herzl Press, January, 1971, Joseph Fraenkel, "German Documents on Zionism," p. 186

81. Abraham Yaari, *The Goodly Heritage, Abridged and Translated by Israel Schen*, Youth Hechalutz Department of the Zionist Organization, 1958, p. 349

Iztchak Shirizli offered a patriotic speech in Turkish, ending with the words, "From this moment we are not separate individuals. All the people of this country are as one man, and we all want to protect our country and respect our empire."[82]

Furthermore, as the war progressed, many had hoped that the German incursion into Poland would liberate the Jews, and victorious Turkey, as a German ally, would then agree to establish Palestine as a Jewish province.

There were those who did not agree. The Russian journalist and later Zionist leader, Zev Jabotinsky, was convinced from the beginning that the Turks would never assent to any form of Jewish autonomy in Palestine.

It would soon become abundantly apparent that there were ample reasons for the Zionists not to support the Ottoman cause. Djemal Pasha was appointed in Palestine as the governor and Turkish military commander to direct military operations against the British to the south in Egypt. He would soon embark upon a campaign to persecute the Jews of Palestine.

He used the proclamation of war to display his antagonism towards the growing Zionist movement. He soon disarmed the *Shomrim* (Jewish guards) who protected the Jewish communities. He closed the Anglo-Palestine Bank, which was necessary for the growth of the Yishuv. Hebrew street signs were prohibited as well as the use of JNF (Jewish National Fund) stamps bearing images of Zionist leaders which supported Zionist agricultural enterprises. Djemal Pasha also prohibited sale of land to non-Ottoman Jews.[83] The use of Tel Aviv currency was prohibited with the penalty of death.

Djemal Pasha then moved to have Jews expelled from Palestine. His target was those Jews with Russian passports, many of whom were Zionists.

He ordered house searches in Tel Aviv for Zionists.[84] On Tuesday

---

82. 334. Avigail Jacobson, *Empire to Empire: Jerusalem between Ottoman and British Rule*, Syracuse University Press, NY, 2011, p. 27

83. Norman Bentwich, *Palestine of the Jews*, University of Michigan Library, Detroit, MI, 1919, p. 185

84. Abraham Yaari, *The Goodly Heritage*, p. 357

December 15, 1914, gun-carrying police rounded up Jewish residents of the adjacent city of Jaffa along with leaders of the Yishuv.

Regional governor of Jaffa, Beha-ed-Din, expelled the Jews from Jaffa on December 17, 1914. Jews who were not Ottoman subjects, meaning they held foreign – mostly Russian – passports, were ordered to leave by boat at 4:00 p.m. Policemen and soldiers arrested people off the streets, young and old, beat them and dragged them to police buildings. They were not allowed to contact their families, or gather their belongings, or prepare provisions. From there, they were dragged to the customs house and then to boats taking them to the ship. When the ship could not hold all the detainees, many were brought back to shore separating families and children from their parents. Initially, about seven hundred Jews were expelled that day.[85]

Zionist leader, Arthur Ruppin, who would soon be exiled despite being a German citizen, wrote, "I had to watch whole families with their horridly collected belongings – old people, mothers with babies – driven on to a boat in infinite disorder."[86]

The Chacham Bashi, (chief rabbi during Ottoman rule of Jerusalem), Rabbi Nissim Danon, lodged a complaint of the cruelty with Djemal Pasha who threatened him with "deposition from his office if he did not stop interfering."[87]

At the same time, conscriptions were announced. This was a process that would continue every few months. Those who could pay the high fee were exempted, most of the others who possessed no desire to serve in the Ottoman army went into hiding.

As a result of the wartime poverty, Jewish religious institutions and charity funds ceased to exist. The few that remained did so at great deprivation.

Thousands were soon given the choice of accepting Ottoman citizenship and face privations of staying in the land under harsh Ottoman rule as well as the military draft, or leaving at once. In

---

85. Avigail Jacobson, *From Empire to Empire, Jerusalem Between Ottoman and British Rule*, p. 23

86. Arthur Ruppin, *Memoirs, Diaries, Letters*, Herzl Press, 1972, p. 153

87. Anonymous, *Palestine During the War*, Zionist Organization, London, 1921, p. 23

late December, 1914, thousands of Jews fled from their homeland to Egypt.

Those with a stake in the land, who were farmers and producers, were promised release from the military, and were more easily able to remain. Many French, Russian and English citizens fled. Jews who emigrated from Russia and were thus considered the enemy, being of Russian citizenship and also because of their Zionist affiliations, faced expulsion, or fled out of fear of persecution. US Ambassador to Turkey Henry Morgenthau, helped arrange the exit of Jews expelled or fleeing with US warships, the Tennessee and Chester, which were in the Mediterranean to protect US Citizens in the region. The United States, then a neutral party, was able to intervene and assist the local population of Palestine. The refugees were brought to Port Said, Egypt, and then to Alexandria where nearby the British authorities had formed refugee camps.[88]

By late 1914, three quarters of the Jewish refugees in Egypt were originally from Russia, and the rest were Sephardic Jews. The number according to Victor F. Naggiar, chairman of the committee to assist refugees, in a letter to the Jewish Chronicle was 11,277 as of December 31, 1914.[89]

The local Jewish committee, with donations from Jewish communities of Western nations, provided for the community's needs setting up synagogues, a yeshiva, a Talmud Torah, and a kosher kitchen.[90] There, the British provided clothing and other needs.

Others arrived at locations in Europe or as far away as the United States.

Diminished food supplies threatened the remaining Jews of Palestine.

American Ambassador to Turkey, Henry Morgenthau, recognized the deteriorating situation facing Palestinian Jewry from the beginning of the war and had $50,000 in aid sent.[91] The ambassador

---

88. Norman Bentwich, *Palestine of the Jews*, p. 184

89. *LJC*, February 25, 1916, p. 20

90. *LJC*, April 14, 1916, p. 14 Interview with David Levontin, Director of the Anglo-Palestine Fund

91. *LJC*, September 18, 1914, pp. 28–29

had cabled New York philanthropist Julius Rosenwald, requesting the funds stating, "Palestinian Jews facing terrible crisis belligerent countries stopping their assistance serious destruction threatens thriving communities."[92] The intervention of the ambassador on behalf of the Jews of Palestine will spare them from fates that would have been even more severe. It is also reasonable to presume that without the watchful eye of Morgenthau over the Jewish community of Palestine, the Turks and their German allies who then feared neutral America would have dealt with the Jews there with even greater severity.

Hunger significantly increased in Palestine due to the scarcities of supplies during the war. All groups in Palestine were affected – Jews, Muslims and Christians. The hoarding, theft and requisition of supplies by the Turks contributed significantly to shortages. A sea blockade prevented exports of grain, citrus and cotton. Imported items like petroleum were unavailable which made transporting existing food supplies from farms all the more difficult. Supply lines were cut and flour prices surged. Also causing depleted supplies were the Turks cutting down trees limiting the supply of firewood. The Jews in particular were affected by the discontinuation of *Chalukah* relief funds. Starvation became widespread. Typhoid and cholera was rampant. By the end of the war, the number of Jews in Eretz Yisrael was reduced to less than half their pre-war population.

To compound the disaster, harvests during the war were poor and an unprecedented severe infestation of locusts in 1915 caused destruction to the land. The locusts swarmed over everything, further depleting food supplies, including almond orchards and orange groves. They even devoured stalks of wheat.[93]

Due to the suffering, some had referred to Palestine as the "Belgium of the East," referring to the suffering there due to the 1914 German invasion.

One prominent Jerusalem rabbi described the abysmal situation.

The famine and filth in the city, the lack of water and soap in

---

92. Online JDC Archives
93. Yaari, *The Goodly Heritage*, p. 371

homes and elsewhere, and the grubby bread caused an alarming outbreak of typhus. Thousands of Jews fell victim to the disease. Pregnant women miscarried and infants died at a terrifying rate. I happened to see the lists of the Sephardic burial society, and I found that the infant mortality in this community, which in ordinary times was about six to eight a month, rose to one hundred or one hundred twenty per month. People bloated from starvation also died by the hundreds. You would see a Jew, especially among the yeshiva students who had no more income, with visible signs of bloat – the cheeks would swell up – and then, a few days later, we would hear he was no longer living, dead of starvation. Since I was handling the distribution of wheat or flour and bread on behalf of the syndicate, and I kept accurate statistics of the Jewish inhabitants, I was aware of the dreadful reality, that during the war years the number of Jerusalem's Jews dropped by half, from 50,000 when the war broke out to about 25,000 at its end.[94]

In particular, the most susceptible were the old and the weak, and in the holy courtyard of the Rosh Yeshiva, Rabbi Wittenberg, of blessed memory, in the Old City, near the Nablus [Damascus] Gate, every last courtyard resident died; not one survived. Among the courtyard residents were old men from the Chabad *kolel* who had lived there for free and owned the *Hekdesh* [property dedicated for religious purposes].[95]

A journalist at the time wrote,

The roads are lined with starving persons who lie about begging for a mouthful of bread. The poor Jews sell all their belongings and clothes, linen and bed covers, to the soldiers to get a few metalliks for food.[96]

---

94. Moshe Blau, *Al Chomotayich Yerushalayim*, Netzach, Bnei Brak, 1946, p. 54
95. Ibid. p. 55
96. Norman Bentwich, *Palestine of the Jews: Past, Present and Future*, Kegan, Paul, Trench, Trubner, and Co. LTD, London, 1919, pp. 189–190

In the words of Jerusalem Rabbi Solomon Shulman, "Our situation is indescribable. We are practically starving. The prices of food stuffs are unimaginably high. There is profound physical and mental depression. Thousands of Jews are gathered in the streets, longing for bread.[97]

Soup kitchens were set up by a host of organizations to feed the hungry. The American consul Otis Glazebrook, sent to Jerusalem by President Wilson, was instrumental in providing desperately needed aid.[98] Assisting in that effort was the US Ambassador to Turkey Henry Morgenthau, who had supplies shipped directly to the shores of Palestine to aid all its inhabitants in need.

Early in the war aid reached the Jews of Palestine through individual efforts. The Joint Distribution Committee was able to send funds through the American consulate in Jerusalem which was distributed by a local committee.

In June, 1915, the consulate closed and the lifesaving distribution of funds was at risk. At that moment, Solomon Hoofien, the Dutch Chairman of the Board of the Anglo Palestine Bank in Jerusalem agreed to act as the distributor for the JDC. He began to receive funds in August but with no directions of what to do because the secret police intercepted his mail. On his own responsibility he borrowed funds, on the hope that one day he would be reimbursed. He enlisted the help of the Spanish Consul, Count Antonio de Ballobar, who gave him space, protection and information. Until, May 31, 1915, when the Zionist Relief Commission took over after the British occupation, the Joint was able to pass a significant sum of life saving funds under Hoofien.[99]

At the same time, males of draft age went into hiding for fear of being forcibly drafted into the Ottoman army. One could be forced into the military by merely walking down the street and being arrested. The circumstances and conditions facing draftees, especially Jewish ones, were very harsh. Thousands of draft age men – up to

---

97. Solomon Shulman, *The Jewish World*, April 7, 1915, p. 11
98. When America declared war on Germany, Glazebrook was forced to leave Jerusalem, but returned early in 1919.
99. Oscar Handlin, *A Continuing Task*, Random House, New York, 1964, p. 31

forty-five years old – were in hiding. If they were found, the penalties were severe.

In Egypt, many of the exiles not only dreamed of returning to Zion, but they would soon help pave the way for others to return as well.

Chapter 13

A Jewish Army:
The First in Almost Two Thousand Years

A few hundred exiles in Egypt gathered on March 3, 1915, within the Mafruza refugee camp – one of a few set up by the British to house the exiles – to deliberate over a plan to form a Jewish fighting unit that would join the seemingly imminent British incursion into Palestine. One month earlier, the failure of the Turkish assault on the British in the Suez raised the possibility of British military action in the land. Under the leadership of Zionist leaders Joseph Trumpeldor and Zev Jabotinsky, who were exiled from Palestine in December, the decision was to create such a fighting unit despite the fact that most of the Zionist establishment had endorsed neutrality during the war.[100] Furthermore, the idea itself was opposed by many Zionists fearing severe repercussions from Turkish authorities who would further increase the oppression of Palestine's Jews. There was also the concern that the Central Powers very well might win the war and they would have been supporting the wrong side.

British Chief of Staff General John Maxwell, doubting that there would be a Palestine campaign and that regulations forbid foreign nationals from serving into the British military, opposed the idea and suggested the alternative of a unit to transfer supplies by mule for an upcoming campaign in Turkey. The British, although initially hesitant, soon agreed to establish the Zion Mule corps. Jabotinsky saw the idea as degrading, since the troops would be a corps of "*mu-*

---

100. Chaim Weizmann also gave his tacit approval. Other Zionist leaders were still hesitant to take a stand against the Turks.

lateers" or mules, and continued to lobby support for a fighting unit, while Zionist, activist, lawyer and soldier, Joseph Trumpeldor, saw this as an opportunity.

About 500 Jewish refugees from Palestine had initially enlisted due to the urging of Trumpeldor. Some enlisted out of appreciation for being housed by the British and sought to serve under the British flag. Others saw in it an adventure.

The fight that would take place in Gallipoli was considered a gateway into Turkey. It was far away from the aspired Jewish Homeland, far from home to those who had dreamed of fighting for Zion. According to Trumpeldor, what mattered was that they were joining in the allied war effort toward the goal of the liberation of Palestine. To Trumpeldor, the roads to Palestine went through the defeat of the Ottoman Empire, wherever they were located. According to Trumpeldor, "Any front leads to Zion."[101]

Seven hundred and thirty seven men had enlisted and served under the leadership of Lieutenant-Colonel Henry Patterson of Irish Protestant origin, who was a staunch Zionist. When Patterson became ill with a stomach ailment on November 29, 1915, Trumpeldor assumed command as the first Jewish leader of an all Jewish army.

On April 27, 1915, the ZMC arrived at the beaches of the Dardanelles Peninsula located upon a major waterway in Northwestern Turkey, under the roar of artillery, cannons, and machine gun fire. Despite the hardships, they managed to form human chains to handle the terrified mules and transport the supplies to the front lines, braving hillsides, wadis, and trenches into no man's land. Aside from supplying needed ammunition and water along with other supplies, and carrying back the wounded, the ZMC – contrary to official policy – did participate in at least one attack against Turkish lines, which was a success.[102]

Despite all the hardships, the Zion Mule Corps put the notion of a national Jewish army on the map. It represented the very foundation of Jews living as a national entity in Palestine.

Regarding the Muleteers, Patterson offered the highest praise,

---

101. Vladimir Jabotinsky, *The Story of the Jewish Legion*, p. 42
102. Elias Gilner, *War and Hope*, Herzl Press, New York, 1969, p. 59

They have not much military experience or opportunity in their later history. But all the honor to them that they do so well now! If the Jew is trained when young, you can make anything of him, especially if you remind him of the glory of his past and his possibilities today.[103]

He wrote of the beginning of the ZMC,

We had a last big parade, and marched from Wardian Camp for some three miles through the streets of Alexandria to the Synagogue, to receive the final blessing of the Grand Rabbi. The spacious Temple, in the street of the prophet Daniel, was on this occasion filled to its utmost capacity. The Grand Rabbi exhorted the men to bear themselves like good soldiers and in times of difficulty and danger to call upon the Name of the L-rd who would deliver them out of their adversity. His final benediction was most solemn and impressive, and will never be forgotten by those who were privileged to be present.[104]

In reflection, John Henry Patterson the Zionist wrote, "I had to ask myself if it were all a dream."[105]

The Gallipoli campaign was a catastrophic failure for the Entente. Their hope of quickly ending the war by an invasion of Turkey resulted in defeat and very heavy casualties on both sides. Of the 480,000 troops of the Entente, 46,000 were killed and over 200,000 were wounded.

The order to disband the corps came on December 28, 1915. Fourteen had died in action, and over sixty men were wounded. Many others were taken out of commission due to contracting malaria. When asked by the British to go to Ireland to suppress the Irish Easter Rising, they declined, stating that their purpose was to fight the Turks, and not to be involved in suppressing Irish independence.

---

103. *LJC*, March 24, 1916, p. 18

104. John Henry Patterson, *With the Zionists in Gallipoli*, General Books, 2011, p. 59

105. Ibid. p. 57

The dreams of Jabotinsky, Trumpeldor and Colonel Patterson of forming a Jewish Legion remained.

In Great Britain, the disastrous failure at Gallipoli along with the very costly stalemate on the Western Front cost Prime Minister Herbert Asquith his job. In December of 1916, he was replaced by David Lloyd George whose war strategy was very different. To Lloyd George, the path to the defeat of the Ottoman Empire ran through Palestine. That's where the British campaign against the Turks would now commence.

Expulsion from Jaffa

As British forces repelled the Turkish advance upon the Suez in 1915 and would eventually push their way into Palestine, persecutions of the Jews intensified. On March, 28, 1917, the Turkish Governor, Djemal Pasha ordered the forced evacuation of the total remaining populations of Tel Aviv and Jaffa.

Some speculate that Djemal Pasha also sought to prevent efforts by the Jews to spy for the British and thus ordered the evacuation. Given the treatment of the Jewish population by the Turkish authorities, that notion was certainly plausible. It can also be said that it was part of an overall policy to punish the Zionist community for their aspirations. A case in point would be the NILI spy group, which at great sacrifice, were caught assisting British forces by providing valuable information.[106]

Notwithstanding the alliance with Turkey, German Jews spoke out against the evacuation orders. Socialist deputy of the Reichstag Oscar Cohn issued a formal complaint to the German Chancellor in protest. One German Jewish newspaper emphasizing Jewish unity stated, ". . . *all* Jewry must prove that it will not desert the pioneers of our generation in the land of our fathers. We approach all Jewry with an urgent appeal. Help! Help! Quickly! Help with love! Jewry must do its duty."[107]

The Germans did intervene on behalf of the Jews of Palestine at

---

106. Abraham Yaari, *The Goodly Heritage*, p. 384
107. *LJC*, June 22, 1917. p. 10 quoted from Berliner Tageblatt

that moment. A diplomatic movement by the Germans sought to soften the severe blow dealt to the Jews of Palestine. The Pasha was advised not to give the enemy "gratuitous propaganda." Soon after, the Pasha postponed the date for expulsion from March 31, to April 9 – the day after Passover. The farmers were allowed to remain and evacuees were promised free transport facilities.[108] That guarantee was not kept.

On April 1, the order was put into effect, which stated that all had to be out of their homes by the 9th of April, the day after Passover. The Pasha stated that those who did not leave during the Passover holiday would be forced out without their belongings in the days following. The exodus of several thousand began immediately. There was no means of transportation. They could only transport those who could not walk and their belongings in carts. Even before their departure, Bedouin gangs were pillaging their homes, under the complicit eyes of the authorities. It was a pitiful scene. The roads were swarmed with men, women and children, roaming helplessly, starving, homeless, facing attacks by bandits. Some of the young men from local settlements tried to protect them, but with limited success as refugees were found along the roads, murdered.[109]

Along roads north of Jaffa, there were thousands of starving Jews. Bandits harassed the exiles, while some young men of local settlements sought to drive them off. They were arrested by the authorities.[110]

The expulsion of 1917 was described by the British High Commissioner of Egypt, Henry McMahon:

> The whole of the Jewish population at Jaffa was expelled towards the North during Passover. Their property was looted and their homes were sacked, the Turkish authorities conniving at their being robbed while in flight. Thousands of Jews are wandering helplessly on the roads starving, while misery and disease are increased by the overcrowding which prevails in the

---

108. Isaiah Friedman, *Germany, Turkey, and Zionism, 1897–1918*, Routledge Press, New York, 1997, p. 349
109. *LJC*, May 4, 1917, p. 10
110. *The Maccabaean*, May, 1917, p. 240

colonies. Young Jews from Jerusalem were deported in masses northwards, their destination being unknown. Evacuation of the colonies by force is imminent.[111]

Tel Aviv, built up for just eight years into a "Garden City" suburb of Jaffa was sacked and lied in a heap of ruins as did Jaffa and other parts of the Yishuv in the land. Many refugees were found murdered by robbers.[112]

As exiles traveled northwards, a call for assistance was sent to Jewish villages in the Galilee and it was answered promptly.[113]

Many of the refugees scattered to Tiberias, Kfar Saba, Petach Tikvah, Zichron Yaakov, the Galilee, while some wound up in Jerusalem, where three hundred Jews were forced out just weeks earlier.

At that time, assistance was requested from the Jewish communities of the Galilee, who responded with the words, "We are your brothers" helping evacuees leave and to find lodging in communities in the North. Other communities as well opened their doors to refugees saving thousands of lives.[114]

According to the narrative of Menachem Klivner who was put in charge of the evacuees at Kfar Saba,

> Thousands of men, women, and children were sent to undergo the hardships and vicissitudes of exile for no reason. . . . In those times, I saw great powers of endurance displayed among our brethren, and also mutual help – the help extended to brothers in distress by *rachamim bnei rachamim* and then I knew mine is a generous people.[115]

In many of the settlements where the exiles arrived, harassment by Turkish troops continued over time until they were conquered by the British.

---

111. *LJC*, March, 18, 1917, p. 14

112. *LJC*, May 4, 1917, p. 10

113. Abraham Yaari, *The Goodly Heritage*, p. 385

114. Gur Alroey, *Expulsion of the Residents of Tel Aviv and Jaffa Passover 1917, Letters from Meir Dizengoff to the Organization of Galillee Settlements*, Central Zionist Archives, File 141v

115. Yaari, *The Goodly Heritage*, p. 388

The new city of Tel Aviv, which was built up in only eight years was now abandoned, as were the Jewish neighborhoods of Jaffa.

Only after British forces made their way north in October, 1918, would the Jews be able to return to their homes, and continue their lives with the bitter memories of April, 1917. By the *Simchat Torah* holiday, a Jewish presence was reestablished in Tel Aviv. The return had begun.

Political Battle over Zion

In the struggle for Jewish statehood, a dispute between Jews took place on the battlefield of public opinion and within the political theatre of Great Britain.

As the outnumbered British forces were successfully engaging Ottoman Turkish troops in Palestine, Zionists in Great Britain were pressing for a statement from the allied forces regarding a Jewish State. At those critical moments, two small, but very influential groups of British Jews were attempting to impede British intentions to endorse such a statement. The two groups were the Board of Deputies of British Jews, led by Claude Montefiore, and the Anglo Jewish Association, led by Edwin Montag, who was also a member of the British Cabinet, and served as British Secretary of State to India.

The two organizations published a manifesto in the Times of London declaring their position.

Published on May 24, the letter dated from May 17, 1917, opposed Jewish Statehood in Palestine, calling it "an anachronism." The letter denied there was a national character to the Jewish people, "The Jewish religion being the only test of a Jew, a Jewish nationalism cannot be founded on, and limited by, the religion."[116] The letter also expressed concern that Jews would be given special rights and considerations in such a state to the exclusion of others. It was signed by David L. Alexander, president of the Board of Deputies, and Claude G. Montefiore, president of the Anglo-Jewish Association.

The members of the two groups, comfortable and affluent in Great Britain, feared that Zionism, which emphasized Jewish nationalism,

---

116. *London Times*, May 24, 1917, p. 16

would raise charges against the Jews of disloyalty and challenge the position they have achieved in Great Britain.

Although Great Britain's Prime Minister Lloyd George, and Foreign Secretary Arthur Balfour, supported Jewish statehood, the letter posed a challenge to British Jewry. It expressed opposition to Zionism and was made public. An ample response was important to demonstrate that the Jewish community of Great Britain did indeed strongly support Jewish statehood.

Three days later, a letter appeared in the Times of London by Lionel Walter Rothschild, Jewish leader and former member of Parliament, who responded by emphasizing that the views of the anti-Zionists did not represent Jewry, "Our opponents though a mere fraction of the Jewish opinion of the world, seek to interfere in the wishes and aspirations of the larger mass of the Jewish people."[117] Rothschild denied the charges that Zionism impeded upon the rights of non-Jews, "I can only again emphasize that we Zionists have no wish for privileges at the expense of other nations' laities, but only desire to work out our destinies side by side with other nationalities in an autonomous state."[118]

A letter by Great Britain's Chief Rabbi J.H. Hertz appeared on the same page, also emphasizing that the expressed views belonged to a very small minority, "I cannot allow your readers to remain under the misconception that the said statements [are] in the least, the views held by Anglo-Jewry as a whole, or by the Jewries of the Overseas Dominions."[119]

Rabbi Hertz's letter was followed with one by Dr. Chaim Weizmann as chairman of the English Zionist Federation, which concluded by expressing regret "that there should be even two Jews who think it their duty to exert such influence as they may command against the realization of a hope which has sustained the Jewish nation through 2,000 years of exile, persecution, and temptation."[120]

When the war broke out, Rabbi Abraham Isaac Kook, then the

---

117. Ibid.
118. Ibid.
119. Ibid.
120. Ibid.

chief rabbi of the city of Jaffa, was in Europe and unable to return to his home. Rabbi Kook, who eventually accepted a post at the London congregation Machzikei HaDas, authored a vociferous letter addressing the Jewish community of Great Britain. The letter's very title, "Manifesto on National Treachery," suggests his unequivocal condemnation of the opponents of the Balfour Declaration.[121]

The opening lines read, "We protest against those who seek to crush the wonderful completeness of Jews and Judaism. We only know a whole Judaism." Rav Kook cited the sentence from the afternoon Shabbat *Minchah* prayer, which contains the words of the prophet Samuel, "You are One and Your name is One, and who is like Your *one nation* Israel on Earth."[122]

Rabbi Kook warned,

> The entirety of our original soul, cannot, under any circumstance, be divided into such parts as "nationalism" and "religion." The pettiness of those who want to split the completeness of our shining force of life into pieces, tearing off a part here and there, is not only a treachery to Jews but also to all of mankind.[123]

Rabbi Kook did not request, but unapologetically demanded that the world return "that which was stolen from us," and then followed by millennium of oppression. "The sin cries up to the heavens, it must be completely corrected. . . . Without compromise, without flattery – completely."[124] He called upon his fellow Jews at that very crucial hour to "actively and forcibly demand that which is ours."[125] The letter requested that all Synagogue leaders read it aloud on the Sabbath of the reading of the Torah portion of *Beha'alotcha*, the weekly Torah portion which fell out on June 15th of that year.[126]

---

121. HaRav Avraham Yitzchak HaKohen Kook, *Igrot HaR'iyah, Vol. III, (Years 1915–1919)*, Mosad HaRav Kook, Jerusalem p. 109
122. Ibid. p. 110
123. Ibid.
124. Ibid. p. 111
125. Ibid.
126. Ibid.

Rabbi Kook's words and efforts had an impact upon British Jewry as well as members of the British Parliament.

During an ensuing debate in the British Parliament over the Balfour Declaration, several members raised the issue over those Jews in opposition. Labour MP (House of Commons) James Kiley (1916–1922) stood up and asked, "Upon whom shall we rely to decide the religious aspect of this issue – upon Lord Montagu or upon Rabbi Kook, the rabbi of Machazikei HaDat?"[127]

Support in Great Britain for the restoration of Palestine to the Jews was at a critical juncture. Palestine would soon fall under British control and the British would have the authority to proclaim Jewish rights to the land.

British Jewry expressed its support.

Protest letters and statements bombarded the pro-Zionist London Jewish Chronicle from rabbis, readers, community leaders, synagogues and Jewish organizations.

The Council of United Jewish Friendly Societies, representing dozens of organizations, released a statement "expressing profound disapproval of such views, and dissatisfaction at the publication thereof and requests its representatives on the said Conjoint Committee to resign their membership thereof forthwith."[128]

The Jewish Chronicle also carried a letter of resignation from the Board of Jewish Deputies by Orthodox Rabbi E.N. Adler, a letter of protest from the prominent leader of the Spanish Portuguese Synagogue, Rabbi Moses Gaster[129] and an article by Zionist leader and author Harry Sacher, which appeared in the Daily News.[130]

In addition, statements were republished throughout the British press, in favor of a Jewish state.

The opponents managed to exert enough pressure to have the original suggested text of the official declaration by Walter Rothschild, which made references to unlimited Jewish immigration and

---

127. Translated by Pesach Jaffe, *Celebration of the Soul: the Holidays in the Life and Thought of Avraham Yitzchak Kook*, Genesis Jerusalem Press, Jerusalem, 1992, p. 188
128. *LJC*, June 22, 1917, pp. 26, 27
129. *LJC*, Ibid., p. 27
130. *LJC*, Ibid.

Jewish autonomy over the land, replaced with a vague text calling for a "Jewish Homeland in Palestine." That text, soon known as the Balfour Declaration, was published on November 2, 1917.

The voices of British Jewry had spoken and were heard.

NILI

General Edmund Allenby arrived in Egypt on June 27, 1917, still prior to the Palestine campaign achieving victory. His plans of marching his forces up the coast from Sinai into Gaza was opposed by his staff, since they had already failed under his predecessor Archibald Murray. On November 1st or 2nd, 1917, Allenby led troops in taking Gaza, swinging his forces around via the city of Be'er Sheva. The conquest of Jerusalem was just six weeks away.

The necessary intelligence provided which allowed for the Allied victory, came from the spy group NILI, the acronym for *Netzach Yisrael Lo Yishaker* (the Jewish People are eternal, Samuel 1, 15:29). NILI was made up of young Zionists mostly from the town of Zichron Yaakov. Unlike most members of the *Yishuv* who feared the Turks, and would not dare even to consider engaging in such actions, members of NILI saw the defeat of the anti-Zionist Ottoman Turks as essential to any future establishment of a Jewish State. Members of NILI who were aware of the mass murders of Armenians were horrified at that news and also feared the same fate could befall the Jews in Palestine. One member, Sarah Aaronson, had witnessed mass executions of Armenians while on a train crossing through Turkey, which increased the group's determination and committment. Her brother, Aaron Aaronson, a recognized agronomist, had agreed to help Djemal Pasha deal with the crippling locust infestation in Palestine, which would also allow him to track the positions of the Turkish army during his travels around the land. Aaronson finally reached British intelligence officer William Ormsby-Gore, who related Aaronson's findings. In addition, it was Aaronson's recommendation that the British invasion advance towards Beersheba off the coast, in the center of the Negev Desert. He based his recommendation upon a source in *The Jewish War* by Josephus Flavius that there were gardens in that area and hence water sources which are paramount to the success of any military operation in that region. General Allenby heeded his advice and the campaign succeeded.

The NILI operation was uncovered as a carrier pigeon sent with messages landed on the home of a Turkish commander. The group was soon discovered and many of its members died martyr's deaths.

According to Britain's chief of military intelligence, Major General George MacDonough, Allenby's ability to carry out his "daring" campaign in Palestine without "unwarranted risks" owed much to NILI: "Allenby knew with certainty from his intelligence of all the preparations and all the movement of the enemy."[131] Raymond Savage, Allenby's deputy military secretary said, "It was largely the daring work of young spies, most of them natives of Palestine which enabled the brilliant Field-Marshall (Allenby) to accomplish his undertaking so effectively."[132] Ormsby-Gore called NILI, "admittedly the most valuable nucleus of our intelligence in Palestine during the war."[133]

As the British campaign advanced, so too did the hopes of the Zionists.

On November 2, 1917, Lord Arthur Balfour summoned Dr. Weizmann, Rabbi Kook, Lord Rothschild, and other Jewish dignitaries to his office and informed them that a text for a declaration granting Palestine as a homeland to the Jews had been worked out.[134]

The text of the Balfour Declaration.

Foreign Office
November 2nd, 1917

Dear Lord Rothschild,

I have much pleasure in conveying to you on behalf of His Majesty's Government, the following declaration of sympathy with Zionist aspirations which has been submitted to, and approved by, the Cabinet.

131. Douglas J. Feith, *The Jewish Spies Who Helped the British Defeat the Ottoman Empire in World War One*, (*Mosaic Magazine*, September 13 2017)

132. Ibid.

133. Ibid.

134. Rabbi Dov Peretz Elkins, *Shepherd of Jerusalem: A Biography of Abraham Isaac Kook*, Arthur Howe, Bloomington, Ind., 2005, p. 87

His majesty's Government view with favor the establishment in Palestine of a national home for the Jewish people, and will use their best endeavors to facilitate the achievement of this object, it being clearly understood that nothing shall be done which may prejudice the civil and religious rights of existing non-Jewish communities in Palestine or the rights and political status enjoyed by Jews in any other country.

I shall be grateful if you would bring this declaration to the knowledge of the Zionist federation.

Yours,

Arthur James Balfour

During an era of ethnocentrism when empires were crumbling and national entities were striving for their own sovereignty, the Jews were promised Statehood in their eternal homeland. The British motive was most importantly the result of sympathies and support of many within the British Government at the time. It was also to some extent, an act of appreciation for the contributions and sacrifices of NILI. (See NILI above.)

The Balfour Declaration received international support.

United States President Woodrow Wilson expressed his support one month in advance of the British proclamation. Wilson, initially hesitant to support the Declaration was influenced by American Jews and Protestant restorationists who lobbied for a political endorsement of Zionism.[135] In September, 1917, Wilson announced his approval in an open letter to the American Jewish leader, Stephan Wise. His statement in support was instrumental to its success.[136]

France made an official statement in favor of the Balfour Declaration. M. Tardieu, the French High Commissioner to the United States, made a statement from M. Pichon, "our views are essentially the same as the British."[137]

Leaders of Italy and Greece also voiced their support.

---

135. Michael B. Oren, *Power, Faith, and Fantasy: America in the Middle East 1776 to Present*, W.W. Norton and Company, New York, London, 2007, p. 364
136. Ibid.
137. *The Maccabaean* March, 1918, p. 89

The Russian newspaper *Novaya Vremya* which had so often spread anti-Semitic propaganda, claimed that Tsar Nicholas II of Russia, before his fall in March, 1917 had purportedly favored Palestine for the Jews.[138]

Naturally, one would not expect the Germans to support a declaration of their enemy, but it was the idea that won some support.

On November 26, 1917, the German newspaper *Deutsche Montags-Zeitung* expressed support for Jewish statehood, and called upon the Central Powers to endeavor to facilitate this objective.

> There are a thousand and one reasons why the Jewish people are entitled to self-government in Palestine, why they should be granted the opportunity to mold their own destiny in their homeland. It is, therefore, of imperative need, that immediate steps be taken by our Government and our ally, Turkey, towards the creation of a Jewish State in Palestine.[139]

An Armenian representative expressed the support of the suffering Armenian people.

> The Armenians, next to the Jews, are happy over the liberation of Palestine. To them, the British declaration in favor of a Jewish homeland is the best augury that their won national dream is nearing realization. The current number of New Armenia gives the leading position to an editorial entitled, "Palestine and Armenia," which says "any capture of Jerusalem by the British army promises to realize the hopes cherished secularly by the Jewish people for a free home land."[140]

The reaction among Zionists was swift, enthusiastic, and widespread. War weary Jewish communities around the world, paused and celebrated. The American Jewish Zionist Newspaper, the *Maccabaean*

---

138. Israel Zangwell, *The War and the Jews*, p. 309
139. *The Maccabaean*, March, 1918, p. 69
140. *American Jewish Chronicle*, February 22, 1918, p. 428

termed the Balfour Declaration, "The Jewish Magna Carta"[141] and added "but the Dark Age of vain mourning is over and a new dawn has risen, a dawn of hope for nations, for small nations too – like Israel."[142]

A popular Yiddish daily, *Dos Yiddishe Folk*, stated, "for the first time in two thousand years we again enter into the arena of world history as a nation which deserves a national home"[143] The religious Zionist movement, *Mizrachi*, issued the following statement that:

> It seems that the Holy Providence which guided Israel in its long night of exile is about to reward the Jewish people for all their suffering and tribulations, which they have undergone not only during the last few years but through the long bitter exile.[144]

In a New York celebration, thousands of Zionists packed Carnegie Hall to hear impassioned speeches, and thousands more crowded outside in the streets around the building.[145]

Christian Zionists around the world were elated as well.

The *Church Family* newspaper stated,

> It is true twenty years ago the educated Jewry, as well as the majority of Christians, thought the Zionist program to be Utopian and absurd – a movement before its time. They were sure the Turks would never allow the Jews to settle in Palestine. Twenty years, however, have brought many and startling changes, but none more soul stirring and thrilling than this proclamation to restore the Jews to Palestine.[146]

In the *Christian Commonwealth*,

> We welcome the declaration all the more because we, too, have an inborn love for the Holy Land, and because we can so deeply

---

141. *The Maccabaean*, December, 1917, p. 1
142. *The Maccabaean*, March, 1918, p. 89
143. *Dos Yiddishe Folk*, quoted by *The Maccabaean*, March, 1918, p. 89
144. *The Maccabaean*, March, 1918, p. 89
145. *The Canadian Jewish Chronicle*, December 28, 1917, p. 7
146. *LJC*, November 25, 1917, p. 22

sympathize with the Jewish people, whose passionate affection for the land of their fathers has never been torn from their hearts, in spite of centuries of persecution and wanderings.[147]

According to the *Methodist Times*, "Naturally this declaration, which will be celebrated in history, has given the liveliest satisfaction to Jewry throughout the world. The pledge is sagacious as it is opportune."[148]

Major media outlets also reacted with praise for the Balfour Declaration.

According to *The Observer*,

> Nearly two thousand years after the Dispersion, Zionism has become a practical and integral part of all schemes for a new world-order after the war. . . . There could not have been at this juncture a stroke of statesmanship more just or more wise.[149]

In the words of *The Nation*, the declaration emphatically favors, "The establishment in Palestine of a national home for the Jewish people. If we were to analyze this sentiment we should find it at its core the simple and humane instinct of reparation."[150]

The *Edinburgh Evening Dispatch* opined,

> Scattered over the face of the Earth, they turn their eyes daily towards Jerusalem and pray for the day when they will be restored to the land of their origin. We are fighting today not for aggrandizement, nor for the acquisition of territory, but for the liberation of peoples crushed by the tyrant, and there is no just and reasonable demand which would not be sympathetically considered by the British Government. Our progress in

---

147. Quoted from Nahum Sokolow, *History of Zionism, (1600-1918), Vol. II*, Elibron Classics, London, 2006, p. 96
148. Ibid. p. 97
149. Ibid. p. 86
150. Ibid. p. 87

Palestine has awakened in the breasts of the "Chosen People" fresh hopes for the re-establishment of their Fatherland.[151]

The Post, in expressing support for Zionism, also espoused an optimism which was not realized,

> A Palestine re-peopled by a Jewry bound to the Allies, and not least to Britain, by ties of affection for righting the oldest national wrong, would be a friendly neighbor to Egypt and to the newly enfranchised territories abutting upon the Holy Land.[152]

On Sunday evening December 2, 1917, crowds gathered in the London Opera House, which was filled to capacity with over 2,700 in attendance. An overflowing crowd met simultaneously in the Kingsway Theatre of London. The rally was entitled a "Great Thanksgiving Meeting," by the *London Jewish Chronicle* and it featured members of the British Government and leaders of British Jewry.[153]

At the rally, speeches were delivered with the frequent theme portraying the British as liberators of the Jewish people from millennium of suffering. British Member of Parliament Colonel Mark Sykes called the event a "turning point in the history of the whole world."[154] MP Robert Cecil proclaimed, "The keynote of our meeting this afternoon is liberation."[155] MP Herbert Samuel, who would later become the first British High Commissioner over the Middle East, pronounced the words, "Next year in Jerusalem" and decried those who had doubted that the British would issue the promise of Jewish statehood.[156] Dr. Chaim Weizmann, president of the English Zionist Federation, who had an integral role in the promulgation of the Declaration, called upon those present to rise and take an oath,

---

151. Ibid. p. 90
152. Ibid. p. 90
153. *LJC*, December 7, 1914, p. 14
154. Ibid.
155. Ibid.
156. Ibid.

which quoted a passage from Isaiah, "If I forget thee Jerusalem, may my right hand forget its cunning."[157]

Among the speakers was the eminent Rabbi Abraham Isaac Kook, whose message differed,

> I have not come here to thank the British nation, but even more, to congratulate it for the privilege of making this declaration. The Jewish nation is the "scholar" among the nations, the "people of the book," a nation of prophets; and it is a great honor for any nation to aid it. I bless the British nation for having extended such honorable aid to the people of the Torah, so that they may return to their land and renew their homeland.[158]

According to the rabbi, the British need not be thanked for giving the Jews what has been rightfully theirs for over three thousand years, or for offering the Jews the land which was taken from them by Roman conquerors 1800 years earlier.

Rabbi Kook offered recognition to the British but not words of gratitude. If the British offered the pledge, then it fulfilled a role for which it was destined.

The Balfour Declaration granted international legitimacy to Zionism, but it would not be a guarantee.

The *London Jewish Chronicle* poignantly observed in 1917, "Neither England, nor France, nor the United States, can give Palestine to the Jewish people, it must be desired, it must be sought for, it must be earned."[159]

It is often claimed that the British made conflicting promises to both Jew and Arab regarding sovereignty over Palestine.

It has been often alleged that the British had already promised Palestine to the Arabs just prior to the March, 1916, Sykes-Picot agreement which planned the post-war division of Middle East territories between British and French control.

On October 24, 1915, Sir Henry McMahon, the British High

---

157. Ibid.
158. Ibid.
159. *LJC*, May 14, 1917

Commissioner to Egypt acting as an intermediary, promised the Sheriff of Mecca the territories which included the "vilayets of Damascus and Beirut."[160] However, there was no specific mention of Palestine. On July 23, 1937, McMahon reiterated in an article in the *London Times* that he did not promise territories in Palestine to the Sheriff Hussein of Mecca,

> I feel it is my duty to state, and I do so definitely and emphatically, that it was not intended by me in giving this pledge to King Hussein to include Palestine in the area in which Arab independence was promised. I also had every reason to believe at the time that the fact that Palestine was not included in my pledge was well understood by King Hussein.[161]

Emir Feisal who led the anti-Turkish, Arab revolt during the war and was designated the ruler of Syria had actually expressed support for Zionism. He had expected that a Jewish state would be established in the land. On March 1, 1919, Faisal wrote a letter to Professor Felix Frankfurter, a member of the Zionist delegation at the Peace Conference, stating that he regarded the proposals of the Zionists as "moderate and proper."[162] He added that he would do what he could to help them through.[163]

Feisal's position changed and became hostile to Zionism only after he was expelled from Syria by the French in 1920.

According to Winston Churchill who was the British Colonial secretary at this time, it was not until January 20, 1921, that the first suggestion was made by Emir Faisal that an Arab Palestine be included within the territory. The British responded that there were no plans to include an Arab state in Palestine.[164]

Initially, reports suggested that Great Britain intended to keep its' commitments to the Balfour Declaration. *The Maccabaean* reported

---

160. *Palestine Royal Report,* July, 1937, Chapter II, p. 20
161. *London Times,* July 23, 1937,
162. *Jews and Arabs in Palestine; Some Current Questions,* Jewish Agency for Palestine, London, 1936, p. 22
163. Ibid.
164. Ibid.

on a letter received by the Provisional Zionist Committee from the Anglo-Palestine Bank in Jerusalem in which the British reassured to "use its best endeavors" to aid in the establishment of a Jewish State in Palestine.[165]

The Conquest of Jerusalem

Following the critical allied victory at Beer Sheba on October 30, the advance accelerated. Aided by allied forces, the British fought their way through each town pushing out the Turks until they reached Jerusalem.

A London dispatch on November 24 reported that the Mosque containing the tomb of the prophet Samuel was bombarded. The ancient site of Mitzpeh, 5,000 yards west of the Jerusalem-Nablus road had been stormed by the British.[166]

British cavalry fought their way into Jerusalem. In the words of a commander,

> It was the first time the brigade had used their swords. When "charge" sounded, I think every man went stark mad. Guns were belching their shells at us in one sheet of flame and bullets by thousands swept past, but no man seemed to get hit as on we went, with drawn swords flashing in the sun, in a long straight line, horses going like mad and everyone shouting like fury. Now, we could see some of our pals falling, yet straight at the guns we charged. As we came up with the first line of protecting infantry the enemy put up their hands as they stood in the trenches, so we jumped them and were charging at the second line when the first line thought better to their surrender and fired at us from behind. The artillery and machine guns kept firing at us up to the moment we reached them with the sword. It seems marvelous that any of us escaped alive but though our ranks were thinned we took the positions and all the guns and ammunition.[167]

---

165. *The Maccabaean*, March, 1918, p. 89

166. *American Jewish Chronicle*, November 30, 1917, p. 91

167. *American Jewish Chronicle*, February 15, 1918, p. 408

On December 9, as Chanukah was approaching, Turkish forces surrendered. In the battles for Jerusalem, twenty-thousand Turkish soldiers, and three-thousand-six-hundred British and allied troops lost their lives. Two days later, on December 11, the second day of Chanukah, British troops marched into Jerusalem. Allenby humbly entered its walls by foot through the Jaffa gate as the city's thirty-fourth conqueror.

Excited crowds lined Jerusalem's streets to welcome the city's liberators. One woman told a newspaper correspondent, referring to the poverty that afflicted the people, that the Jews "have been starving but now we are free."[168]

One British member of the military described his entry into Jerusalem,

> People of all ages and apparently of all nationalities, thronged the roadway, crowded at their doors and windows, and squeezed themselves on the roofs of their houses. Swarms of children, Arab, Jew, and Christian, ran with us as we marched along, and the populace clamored to any point of vantage, waving and clapping their hands, cheering and singing. Jews clad in European dress came running up, singled out any one of us, wrung him by the hand, and –talking excitedly in broken English – said that they, the people of Jerusalem, had been waiting for that two-and-a-half years. Never was a welcome made more manifest than that accorded to the British troops on the occasion of the delivery of Jerusalem from the bonds of Turkish oppression.[169]

A Jewish periodical, The *London Jewish Chronicle*, headlined the event as "The Rising of Jerusalem," describing the allied conquest as an "Epochal event" and stated with mystic overtone, "It is as if Providence had placed its blessing upon an enterprise distinguished as had been the Palestine campaign by the historic [Balfour] declaration to

---

168. *LJC*, December 14, 1917, p. 14

169. Bernard Blaser, *Kilts Across the Jordan*, H.F.& B. Witherby, London, 1926, p. 120

the Jewish people."[170] Rabbi J.H. Hertz, Chief Rabbi of the British Empire forwarded a telegram to General Allenby that read, "British Jewry thrilled by glorious news from Palestine, sends heartfelt congratulations on historic entry into Holy City."[171] Rabbi Hertz also issued a statement linking the British entry into Jerusalem which occurred during the holiday of Chanukah,

> Jerusalem which for ages has been the majestic pole of love and reverence of the world is now in British hands. And this soul thrilling news reaches us on the day that the Jews are celebrating the Maccabean festival. On this day 2,080 years ago the Maccabees freed the Holy City from the heathen oppressor and thereby changed the spiritual future of humanity. Who knows but that today's victory may form as a glorious landmark in the history of mankind.[172]

Zionist leader Chaim Weizmann who played a significant role in the negotiations leading to the issuing of the Declaration, phoned the *London Jewish Chronicle* and stated, "The news of the British victory will raise the hopes of Jews all over the world. It opens the prospects of the realization of hopes which have existed in their kinds for centuries."[173]

According to one American Jewish periodical, the Turks placed dynamite charges in flour mills in Jerusalem to prevent the distribution of bread, just prior to their evacuation. The arrival of the British saved the people from total starvation by advancing 25,000 pounds to S. Hoofian, who had managed to evade the authorities and tried to keep people fed.[174]

Before the surrender, American nationals in Jerusalem had fled. With the approach of the British, men came out of their hiding places to protect the women from Turkish brutality as women and

---

170. *LJC*, December 14, 1917, p. 14

171. Ibid.

172. Ibid.

173. Ibid.

174. *American Jewish Chronicle*, March 29, 1918, p.617

children felt threatened. Word rang out, "The English are coming." The British had fled (in fear) with the 62 men.[175]

On the day of the taking of Jerusalem, the citizens of the city woke up early and went out to the streets, first with hesitation; just to see if indeed the Turkish front fell. Then as if in a dream, to see the crowds, emerging from their "holes" and all marching west (to Jaffa Gate) to witness the ceremony in which the city is passed to the British conqueror. And then the city was joyful and rejoiced.[176]

In the first month after the "Redemption of the city," not much had changed. The residents had not yet recovered from the famine, and were not healed from their sicknesses. Young school students were still distant from their parents in the fighting countries. Everybody was waiting for additional aid that would hopefully come from afar.[177] In the meantime, the communication with the Tel Aviv-Jaffa residents was renewed. They were liberated a few weeks before Jerusalem was freed.[178]

At the early reopening of the Jaffa bank, with the British capture of Palestine, it was reported that the British government made deposits in the bank, and had been invited to make foodstuff purchases for the civilian population of Jerusalem.[179]

The British military soon appointed Ronald Storrs to make sure the people of Jerusalem were provided with necessities which became even more increasingly scarce as Turkish forces fled Jerusalem. With the assistance of General Allenby, Storrs imported enormous supplies of wheat from Egypt each month. He made sure pipes were installed so water could be brought into Jerusalem. He also fixed prices so opportunists would not take advantage. Also, efforts were made to improve public health. Public garbage bins were installed, the entire population was vaccinated against small pox and pools of water were covered and sprayed to prevent malaria.[180]

---

175. Ibid. February 15, 1918, p. 408

176. David Benveniste, *HaGedud HaIvri: Bimei Milchemet HaOlam HaRishona: Yoman*, Bit'on HaTzibur HaSephardi Va'Edot HaMizrach, Jerusalem, 1977, p. 5

177. Ibid. p. 6

178. Ibid.

179. *The Maccabaean*, March, 1918, p. 89

180. Bar Ilan University, *Jerusalem: Life Throughout the Ages in a Holy City, Inter-*

It would take time for the city to recover. The infrastructure of the city began to be revitalized. New infrastructures and facilities were constructed. Another sign of growth was the cornerstone to the future Hebrew University was laid upon its future site on Mount Scopus on April 10, 1918. At the ceremony, Dr. Chaim Weizmann spoke of goals to be achieved by the Zionist movement,

> In order to make the declaration into reality we have to unite all our nation's efforts in the land and in the Diaspora, in preparing the land to massive settlement and quick organization of the Hebrew Battalions that will participate in conquering the rest of the land.[181]

Seventy-five years later Anna-Grace Lind would again watch General Allenby stride into Jerusalem. This time, Viscount Allenby, the general's great nephew, entered the city with Jerusalem's Mayor Teddy Kollek. Events commemorated the 75th anniversary of Ottoman surrender to the British. Kollek stated, "The British were welcomed equally by Jews, Christians, and Muslims, all of whom suffered under 400 years of Turkish rule."[182]

Fighting for Jewish Statehood

After intense lobbying, British military leaders relented and allowed the formation of what would be known as the Jewish Legion. The Jewish army was composed of Jews around the world to join the allied fight in the conquest of Palestine. Despite virulent opposition within the Jewish establishment including some prominent Zionists, Jabotinsky's dream became a reality.

There were many opponents as there was fear of the potentially severe repercussions at the hands of the Turks.

The opposition extended beyond Palestine. The following let-

---

net *Educational Activities*, May 1997, David Eisenstat, 12/12

181. David Benveniste, *HaGedud HaIvri: Bimei Milchemet HaOlam HaRishona: Yoman*, Bit'on HaTzibur HaSephardi Va'Edot HaMizrach, Jerusalem, 1977, p. 14

182. *JTA*, December 10, 1992

ter was similar to others which expressed the concern that with the formation of the Jewish Legion the Jews would be viewed as pariahs within their respective societies.

> As a Jew and a Zionist, I read it as my duty to protest with all my power against the formation of the Jewish regiment and against the idea of sending it to Palestine. Jews fight not as Jews but as residents of their countries.[183]

The first battalion, known as the 38th, was composed of Russian Jews in Great Britain, many known as the "tailors," given their common occupation. It was commanded by Colonel John Henry Patterson, who had previously commanded the Zion Mule Corps.

On February 3, 1918, the 38th battalion of the Jewish regiment marched through West London to cheers. "Among the spectators were many Jews of the London East Side, duly elated and proud. The Jewish quarter was decorated with Zionist flags. The Batallion carried the Union Jack and two Zionist flags with the *Magen David* bearing the Hebrew inscription, "If I forget thee, O' Jerusalem, let me right hand forget its cunning." The military bands played *Hatikvah*."[184]

Two days later, they left for Palestine.

Zev Jabotinsky described that event.

> Tens of thousands of Jews [are] in the streets, at the windows and on the roofs. Blue-white flags were over every shop door; women crying with joy, old Jews with fluttering beards murmuring *Shehecheyanu*; Patterson on his horse, laughing and bowing, and wearing a rose which a girl had thrown to him from a balcony; and the boys, those "tailors," shoulder to shoulder, their bayonets dead level, each step like a single clap of thunder, clean, proud, drunk with the national anthem, with the noise of the crowds, and with the sense of a holy mission. . . . Long life to you, my "tailors" of Whitechapel and Soho, Leeds and Manchester! You were good tailors: you found the torn rages

---

183. *LJC*, August 17, 1917, p. 15, Letter, "A Protest"
184. *The Maccabaean*, March, 1918, p. 89

of Jewish honor and sewed them together – to make a beautiful and everlasting flag.[185]

The 2nd battalion, the 39th, was formed in America. Some of its members were Palestinian Jews who took refuge in America during the war. It was under the command of Lieutenant-Colonel Eliezer Margolin, a Zionist leader, who earned distinction during several allied campaigns.

In America, on account of age and alien citizenship, and therefore not eligible to serve US armed forces, (as in Great Britain), troops with US and Star of David flags marched through Manhattan in honor of Jewish legionnaires on their way to fight.[186]

There was American support for the Jewish legion. Though federal law forbade foreign armies recruiting on American soil, the Wilson administration raised no objection when Jabotinsky began to enlist American Jews.[187]

Both these battalions saw action on the Palestine front: The 38th and 39th saw action in September, 1918 on the Eastern front of the Palestine campaign taking Es-Salt,[188] thousands of Turkish and hundreds of German prisoners. Several dozen members of the battalion were lost in the campaign.

The 3rd battalion, the 40th, was recruited in Palestine under the British occupation, while parts of the land were still in Turkish hands. But it was formed too late to take an active participation in the fighting.

Meetings in Jerusalem: Formation of the Jewish Legion in Palestine

On Jan. 11, 1918, the first meeting took place in the *Hapoel HaTzair* (The Zionist Young Worker) branch in Jerusalem. The meeting was

---

185. Jabotinsky, *The Story of the Jewish Legion*, p. 104

186. *The Maccabaean*, May, 1918, p. 130

187. Oren, *Power, Faith and Fantasy*, p. 363

188. Es Salt is a town West Central Jordan which was the scene of two battles between the Allies and the Turks in the spring of 1918. The allies triumphed over the retreating Turks.

about the volunteering for the Jewish Legion.[189] The debate reflects the differences of opinion on the merits of joining the Jewish Legion.

The head speaker was Yitzchak Wilkansky from Tel Aviv, who spoke about the arguments between the workers and the students in Tel Aviv and the farmers in the cooperatives (*moshavim*). There were two groups, he said; "The Activists" who see the need for the "Jewish Legion" and the *metunim* (moderates) who reject the idea for security reasons. They considered the notion to be dangerous, and believed that it was necessary to manage what was already achieved, and concentrate upon improving their financial situation, which was imperiled by the war. Most of the rejecters were members of *Ha'Poel HaTzair*.[190]

There was support. The registration in Tel Aviv still continued and many of the *Gimnasya* (High School) students, workers and farmers sons (especially from Rechovot) showed their willingness to be recruited. The excitement was great when it was known that one of the *Gdudim Ivrim* (Jewish brigades) would soon be arriving.

There was a reception in support at the board of volunteers from Tel Aviv with Moshe Smilansky of Rechovot, a Zionist activist who arrived in Palestine in 1890. Smilansky spoke out against the "Rejecters" stating that there was no value to maintain the existing status quo if it is in the hands of a government that is hostile to Jewish rights in the land. "We can have the "National Home" (*Beit Leumi*), but we are required to participate in obtaining the land upon which it is going to be built."[191]

He added, "Our participation will be by joining the British war effort by creating a Hebrew battalion that will be added to the other Hebrew battalions that are being organized in England and the United States."[192]

Berl Katznelson, one of the fathers of the *Histadrut*, (Zionist labor union), said that the Jewish Legion "is needed at the moment, just

---

189. David Benveniste, *Gedud HaIvri*, p. 13
190. Ibid. p. 14, *HaPoel HaTzair* are the Young Workers Party.
191. Ibid. p. 8
192. Ibid.

like the idea of work in the settlements at the time; this idea will be, with time, a part of the values we build upon our land."[193]

One of the instructors in the school for teachers announced,

> My three sons were designated to be sent to the Turkish army. This time I'm sending them to the Hebrew army. Blessed will be them if they will go and fulfill their holy obligation and cursed will be them if they won't go. Blessed will be all the students who will leave their books and notebooks and volunteer to the "Jewish Legion."[194]

Among those who supported the Jewish Legion, there were those who wanted to sign up immediately, and those who conditioned their registration upon the approval of the *Histadrut Ha'tzionit* (central labor union) to supporting the Legion. It was agreed to continue the meeting the following day.[195]

In actuality, no official approval was required. A decision was made to volunteer "unconditionally," (without approval from the *Histadrut*). On that same day fifty students from the higher grades of the high school, 20 of them from the teachers school, along with some elementary teachers and 15 of the city's educated men [all volunteered].[196]

A few demands were put together that the volunteering committee must bring to the attention of the British headquarters:

1. The volunteers will join the troops that will fight only to redeem the land of Israel.
2. *Hagedud Ha'Ivri* will be marked on the military uniform by wearing a *Magen David* (Star of David) symbol.
3. The commands will be given in Hebrew.
4. The flag will have a Jewish star
5. It is advisable that the commanders will be Jewish.

---

193. Ibid.
194. Ibid.
195. Ibid.
196. Ibid. p. 9

The commitment includes service until all of the land of Israel is conquered. At the end of the war the Jewish Legion will become a Hebrew militia. Its task will be to guard the land.[197]

On Feb. 16, 1918, at the first convention of the volunteers' movement, Zev Jabotinsky spoke about the Jewish Legions organizing in England and the US.[198] Jabotinsky who faced a torrent of opposition remained firm, telling the audience, "There is but one truth in the world, and it is all yours. If you are not sure of it, stay at home; but if you are sure, don't look back, and it will be your way.[199]

On March 25, 1918, the 40th Division of the Jewish Legion in Palestine was formed.

At a subsequent volunteers meeting in Jerusalem, Jabotinsky expressed the need for self-reliance among Zionists,

> We can't count on the English Government's and the other governments' promise. We have to show the world that we have the power and the willingness to recruit battalions within us that will fight back to back with the British army in redeeming the land of Israel from the Turkish.[200]

He added that the official recruiting day will be on April 4, 1918. On that day all the volunteers will gather in Rechovot, go through a military physical check-up and it's possible that they would then be sent to Egypt for training.[201]

Jabotinsky mentioned the words of Chaim Weizmann: "If we had the armed forces at the time of the negotiation over the Balfour's declaration, our achievements would have been greater and the declaration would have had a greater political significance."[202] He concluded with the words "see you in the battlefront."[203]

---

197. Ibid.
198. Ibid.
199. Vladimir Jabotinsky, *The Story of the Jewish Legion*, Bernard Ackerman, New York, 1945, p. 63
200. Benveniste, *Gedud Ha'Ivri*, p. 12
201. Ibid.
202. Ibid.
203. Ibid.

Conspicuously missing at the meeting was General Allenby, which was considered a big disappointment.[204]

Hadassah

An aspect in the rebuilding of Zion was the participation of American Jews to provide assistance and badly needed healthcare to the residents of the *Yishuv*. Procuring medicines during the war was extremely difficult. According to the *London Jewish Chronicle*, "Prices have risen four times the normal. Medicines cannot be obtained. Conditions are worse than we can portray them."[205]

Amid the health crisis in Palestine, American Jews and other Jewish communities abroad began to intensify mobilization to provide for the health needs of the people. It was during the First World War that the activities of Hadassah intensified.

As the Jewish Legions were formed, a Hadassah group from New York of thirty doctors and nurses arrived with medicines and the promise of millions and billions of dollars to come for the building of the Jewish State.[206]

A medical unit was organized and clinics were set up for childbirth, children's diseases, and the distribution of medicines and milk.[207]

At the beginning of the war, two nurses were sent into the Old Yishuv and acted as midwives where there was a desperate need. When the two nurses were forced to leave in 1915, replacements were sent. Also one was sent to Alexandria to tend to the refugees. Of the doctors, nurses and orderlies passing through London on their way to Palestine on an "errand of mercy . . . their first effort on arrival was the establishment of a hospital of one hundred beds. But this mission has, apart from all else, a great practical value in the era of reconstruction upon which Palestine is now entering."[208]

Following the British occupation, the work of Hadassah increased.

---

204. Ibid.

205. *LJC*, July 13, 1918, p. 6 "The Hadassah Unit"

206. Jabotinsky, *The Jewish Legion*, p. 121

207. *The Maccabaean*, February, 1917, p. 147 Hadassah in Palestine, Henrietta Szold,

208. *LJC*, July 13, 1916, p. 6

British authorities in Jerusalem allowed Hadassah's work to continue in the *Le'maan Zion* (for the sake of Zion) Hospital instead of requisitioning the premises for military use. The hospital was actually owned by a German organization. British military authorities recognized the work of Hadassah. They permitted Dr. Bertha Kagan, in charge of Hadassah operations in Jerusalem, to continue her work at the *Le'maan Tzion* hospital in Jerusalem. "The building which is property of a German organization became formerly known as Hadassah hospital. Hadassah, lifesaving work is also helping starving children and is now becoming a national organization."[209]

Funds from around the world increased for Hadassah hospital after a three year struggle. In the words of one doctor, "Now at last my dream is realized. I take the little poor body, famished and undermined by sickness, into my care and soon I see its features become reanimated, and I see it smile, perhaps for the first time in its life. Unfortunately, we are unable to give them clothing because we have none."[210]

The following is a report of the Hadassah Medical Unit passing through Great Britain on its way to Palestine in 1918.

The medical unit of Hadassah, which is passing through this country from America on its way to Palestine, received a hearty welcome at the Savoy last Monday, and the greeting will be cordially re-echoed throughout the community. The doctors, nurses and orderlies who compose the Unit are proceeding to the ancient land on an errand of mercy; their first effort on arrival is to be the establishment of a hospital of one hundred beds. But this mission has apart from all else, a great practical value in the era of re-construction upon which Palestine is now entering. The community of America, with the good sense which is its characteristic, [states] that one of the first steps towards making Palestine a prosperous country is to make it a clean and healthy country.[211]

---

209. *American Jewish Chronicle*, April 12, 1918, p. 657
210. Ibid.
211. *LJC*, July 13, 1918, p. 6

Hadassah also had clothing items sent to Palestine. Hundreds of volunteers canvassed department stores and manufacturing houses securing contributions of garments.[212]

From His Attic to the Jewish Legion

Yeshiva student Aaron Werner, like many young men, hid from Turkish authorities in 1917 to avoid the draft. He spent much of his time in an attic as he continued his study of Talmud. Once, while Aaron was attending a Synagogue in Petach Tikva, the Turkish police descended upon the worshippers. The young ones among them escaped through the windows and hid in the nearby olive groves. When the police left, the boys returned to their hiding places.

Aaron was the youngest member of the *Hevra Kadisha*, the Jewish burial society, and helped bury many Jewish victims of the Cholera and Typhus epidemics. When the British army occupied Jerusalem, Aaron left his attic and joined the Jewish Legion, in which he served with distinction.[213]

Determination

Sergeant G., a thickset little man with a neck like a bull, a costermonger in the Ghetto, who had joined at the commencement of the war, fought in France, and came to the Judeans shortly after it was started. In the days of training, he had not impressed any of us very strongly except as a professor of a varied repertoire of comic songs sung in a stentorian voice, and of a reputation as a doughty fighter in the ring. When we were on a long march to Es Salt and the men were dog-tired, hungry, and faint with thirst, G. came to his own; he sang when the other had their tongues lolling out of their mouths: when singing ceased to inspire, I actually saw him dancing a hornpipe

---

212. *American Jewish Chronicle*, February 22, 1918, p. 428

213. Roman Freulich, *Soldiers in Judea: Stories and Vignettes of the Jewish Legion*, Herzl Press, New York, 1964, p. 76

with his pack on up the never ending-ascent. On the way back he developed dysentery and I ordered him to the hospital. He refused to go and marched on. Suddenly, I found him lying on the side of the road too weak to move. I had nothing to do but leave him with some pills. At the next station, he had caught up – again he dropped, but he would not give in and again he struggled on to Jerusalem. There he worked like a Trojan. He fed the sick, shaved them, sang to them till he too went down with Malaria, but even then he would not just lie down for a few hours while the rigor was on and then be up again working away and cheering up the poor sick fellows. Eventually, I pushed him into hospital.[214]

Accounts from the Jewish Legion

There are several accounts of troops during the Jordan River campaign of the Jewish Legion in 1918, who prayed on Yom Kippur despite the proximity of the enemy.

Phillip Brodsky, the company cantor was wide awake. He was well aware that this night was Yom Kippur. Completely forgetful of the order to be silent, he softly began to chant *Kol Nidrei*. Emotion choked every word, making the chant more poignant. Several other soldiers joined in, and within a few minutes, all the soldiers were singing in unison, completely oblivious of the captain's command. Suddenly, the translucent and magical singing was shattered by distant shots. Captain Smalley awoke. He crawled out of his pup tent. There was amazement on his face. He stood motionless, gazing in the direction of the singing soldiers, his heart filled with admiration. When the singing ended, he returned to his tent and peacefully went back to sleep.[215]

One Jewish prisoner, a native of Tiberias, had his four-year-

---

214. Radcliffe Solomon, *Palestine Reclaimed*, G. Routledge & Sons, New York and London, 1920, p. 98

215. *Soldiers in Judea*, p. 108

old son with him. Three years earlier, he had been conscripted into the Turkish army and had served on many fronts. A few months before being taken prisoner he was transferred with his regiment to the Palestinian front. Fortunately, he found himself near Tiberias, and managed to visit the city of his birth. He searched for his wife only to learn that she was dead. With the help of a Jewish merchant, he found his son, starving and homeless. He took the child with him, and the boy became the mascot of the regiment. Eventually, the man joined the Legion and his son was placed with a Jewish family in Rishon Lezion.[216]

Passover for the Jewish soldiers serving in Egypt has been a very happy and successful feast in all respects ... In the closing speeches we "toasted" our brethren on all fronts, and the only regret was for those in this force whose duty prevented them from being with us. As the stirring strains of *Hatikvah* rang out at the end, after "G-d save the King," our hopes waxed high that we should soon re-enter our own Holy City – Jerusalem – of which we had been thinking so much throughout the feast.[217]

Fighters of the Jewish Legion were sent on a mission to Damascus to deliver supplies to the British. They arrived on the eve of the Sabbath. The following event is recalled on March 1, 1919.

We woke up early and left the station towards the Jewish quarter. The city was still sleeping ... We were afraid of an enemy ambush ... We cocked our weapons just in case ... suddenly a door opened and out came a bearded Jew with Shabbat clothes, and his *Talit* bag under his arm. He stood still and wondered amazed, "*Shalom Aleichem, Shabbat Shalom* Rabbi." He came closer and saw the *Magen David* on our arms. He approached and kissed it with excitement and then called out loud: "Jewish soldiers! Jewish soldiers! Welcome! *Shabbat Shalom U'Mevor-*

---

216. Ibid. p. 101
217. *LJC* 5.11.17 p. 18, reported from Cairo by Rev Simon Grajowsky

ach!" From all the windows and doors came out Jews on their way to the synagogue, they escorted us all the way to their synagogue, set us next to the eastern wall and called us for an *Aliyah* (reading of the Torah portion), as customary with important guests.[218]

---

218. David Benveniste, *Gedud Ha'Ivri*, p. 36

Chapter 14

Aftermath of the Armistice

On November 11, 1918, 11:00 AM, an agreement signed between the Entente and Germany at Compiegne France, ended hostilities on the Western front and signified the end of the First World War.

What kind of world would follow the war?

The hope was that with the end of the war, democracy and freedom would advance. That good sense and judgement would prevail and replace the madness of the Great War.

Such would not happen.

American President Wilson had called it the "war to end all wars." He promoted fourteen points for peace, which included the establishment of the League of Nations as an international forum to resolve disputes. Wilson, as other leaders at the time, also believed that liberating smaller nations from the control of empires which had fallen during the war would promote peace. The President's plans had received international support although not from his own congress, but the peace for which he had hoped, was not forthcoming. Wars soon broke out throughout Europe as smaller nations arose like Czechoslovakia, Austria, Hungary, Lithuania, Poland, Ukraine, Latvia, Estonia, Finland, Yugoslavia and Armenia. As a result, dangerous ethnic-nationalisms were unleashed and conflict ensued. The resulting tensions often threatened Jews throughout Europe.

There was also hope that nations would guarantee the rights of Jewish minorities throughout Europe.

At the Versailles conference in 1919, terms of surrender were negotiated with Germany as well as conditions for post-war Europe.

The negotiations which lasted for months included the establishment of nations following the breakup of empires due to the war. Minority rights were sought as a means of internal peace in multinational states.

Jewish activists arrived to press the case for Jewish rights in their countries of origin. Jewish delegates pushed for the protection of Jews and new states. They requested that Jews be granted some forms of autonomy for their own safety.

In 1914, Jews on all sides enthusiastically answered the call to arms and served with distinction but ultimately that did little to ameliorate the growing isolation felt by the Jewish community as global anti-Semitism again was on the rise.

The time of hope soon dimmed after WWI and gave way to pessimism. The tone turned ominous with pessimistic premonitions among the Jews as to their future post-war status.

In Germany, Jews faced accusations of betrayal. Since the war-fronts were far off and out of Germany, the perception of many Germans was that Germany really did not lose the war but was actually betrayed. It was referred to as the "stab in the back" theory which implied that German Jewry as well as other minorities had betrayed their fatherland by allegedly plotting and pressing at home for surrender during times of unrest in Germany near the end of the war while the troops languished at the front. The reality was that Germany was defeated and its army faced collapse. Such spurious accusations outraged German Jews but little could be done to persuade anti-Semites otherwise.

It was actually German Jewry that was being viciously stabbed in the back.

The following are a few of the expressions reflecting the pessimism felt by many Jews following the war.

Over Two Years before Armistice

The Jewish Criterion quoted the editor of the *Jewish Advocate*, Jacob DeHaas opined in 1916, "The rising tide of chauvinism is everywhere promoting a fresh anti-Semitism. The reward of the Jews for bravery and patriotism will, within Europe, be hatred. This is not prophesy, the facts lie too near fulfillment for any such claim."[219]

An editorial in the American Jewish Chronicle observed,

> It is assumed even by Jewish optimists that the conclusion of this war will see the rise of anti-Semitism everywhere. The masses or the classes always need a scapegoat for every evil that comes upon them, and the scapegoat is always found in the politically weak. We already see anti-Jewish feelings spreading in many belligerent countries.[220]

Looking to the future, in a weekly column for a Jewish periodical known as *The Communal Armchair*, the article entitled, "Live Together or Die Together" by an anonymous columnist, ominously predicted, "It is manifest that the air raids of the Great War, to just give an instance of the multiplying of the murder enterprise, compared with the air raids of the next war, will seem as a pop gun with a rifle."[221]

On November 22, just days after the armistice, pogroms in Poland erupted in the city of Lvov. Ukrainian forces attempted a coup in parts of recently declared independent Poland which also encompassed Eastern Galitzia containing a large population of ethnic Ukrainians. As Polish forces forced the withdrawal of Ukrainians from Lvov, a mob of soldiers and civilians made their way to the Jewish quarter of the city and proceeded to destroy Jewish property and attack Jews. Most of the Jews of Galitzia did not want to take sides and were thus subject to accusations of treason. In the ensuing violence, between seventy-three and one-hundred-fifty Jews were murdered and four hundred and sixty three were wounded.[222] The incident which was publicized around the world was the first disaster of many that the Jews of Europe would endure following the war. As the German military presence withdrew from the Eastern front after the war, open hostilities broke out against the Jews.

---

219. *The Jewish Criterion*, quoted March 3, 1916, Issue No. 27, p. 7
220. *American Jewish Chronicle*, March 22, 1918, p. 547
221. *LJC*, "In the Communal Armchair" September 15, 1922, p. 9
222. Alexander Prusin, *Nationalizing a Borderland*, p. 85

Pogroms would soon break out in Vilna, Pinsk, and other cities due to unrest as Polish soldiers were engaged in battles against communist revolutionary forces as part of the ongoing post revolution effort by communists to control Russian Republics. Pogroms also broke out in Czechoslovakia and Hungary due to unrest.

The Horrors of the Haidamaks

Haidamaks were bands of Cossacks. In the Ukraine, Cossack forces again marched against the Jews, and they inflicted atrocities on a massive scale in 1919.

A major catastrophe struck the Jews of Ukraine. It was perhaps the worst slaughter since the destruction of the Judean state by the Romans in the first and second centuries. As German forces withdrew from Ukraine following the war, Ukrainian nationalists in an effort to oust the Bolshevik regime, took control over the Ukraine and established a "Directory" whose government was in the city of Kiev. The revolutionary Bolsheviks, otherwise known as the Red Army, countered their efforts. The white Russians, who sought to re-establish the rule of the Czars, also intervened, marching from the south through the Ukraine to topple the Soviet regime in what was a raging civil war. Amid the turmoil, Jewish communities comprising two million Jews were targeted by all three opposing forces, although the least brutal were the Bolsheviks. Bogus accusations arose among the Ukrainian nationalists and White Russians, that because some of the Bolshevik leaders were Jewish, the Jews as a whole were Communists.

The Ukrainian nationalist forces under the leadership of Simon Petlura perpetrated over 685 pogroms. Under Anton Denikin, while the White Russians crossing the Ukrainian frontier were guilty of perpetrating over 200 pogroms, the Bolsheviks were also engaged in committing excesses. Estimates of casualties differed. Tens of thousands were murdered in pogroms, although some estimates run much higher. As pogrom survivors fled the carnage, they often perished from starvation and disease. This catastrophe which was comparable to the anti-Jewish massacres in the Ukraine perpetrated by the Cossacks under Bogdan Chmielniski in 1648–1649, and under

Ivan Gonta in the middle of the 18th century in the city and vicinity of Uman, was a direct consequence of the First World War and the fall of the Russian Czar.

The horrors which have been well documented, defy description and foreshadowed the mass murder of the Nazi holocaust.

The 1919 report by the Committee of the Russian Red Cross of Kiev stated,

> The recent epidemic of pogroms is distinguished from those that preceded it, first by its long duration and then by its refined cruelty, by the merciless thoroughness and naked blood thirstiness with which the crime was carried out.[223]

The International Red Cross reported that:

> Hundreds of thousands of Jews have been robbed of their last shirt, hundreds of thousands have been maltreated, wounded, humiliated; tens of thousands have been massacred. Thousands of Jewish women became victims of bestial instincts of savage hordes. . . . The Jewish masses in the Ukraine are on the verge of madness and many have actually lost their reason. These unfortunate beings, having lost all that makes life worth living, their nearest, their homes, everything they had, all means of existence, mutilated physically and broken morally, how can they solve the problem of their existence? Where are they to find shelter? How to save the children from dying of starvation and cold, and all the accompanying miseries?[224]

In a contemporary article on the horrors of Ukraine, the estimate is given of 80,000 people killed.

> But when the full reports have been gathered, in it will be found that an enormous number of people have been slain. According

---

223. Ismar Elbogen, Translated by Moses Hadas, *A Century of Jewish Life*, Jewish Publication Society of America, Philadelphia, PA, 1946, p. 497
224. Ibid. pp. 499–500

to the estimate of the administration in the various parts of the country about a hundred thousand have been killed. The Jewish estimate, however, is 250,000; this includes the results of the massacres in other districts not under the dominion of the Ukrainians.[225]

The report continued, "In many places, I may tell you that not a single Jewish resident is left – all have been killed or have escaped to another part of the country."[226]

The *New York Times* quoted an article from the Yiddish daily, *Der Tog*, "The Day," which stated that the anti-Jewish events in the Ukraine,

> "Leave the scope of ordinary pogroms and assume the character of a slaughter which will forever be written in letters of blood on the pages of Jewish history."[227]

At a meeting held in Philadelphia in protest of the slaughter, Archbishop Dougherty of the Roman Catholic Church described the horrors and referenced the town massacre of Proskurov,[228] on February 15, 1919, quoting an American correspondent of various newspapers.

> It was carried out systematically and according to a prearranged plan. The Cossacks did not skip a single house in the Jewish quarter. Entire blocks with all their inhabitants were annihilated. The murderers would not permit their victims to die an easy death. They made sport of them. They tormented and subjected them to a slow torture. They used no firearms. They economized on bullets, strangled their victims with their hands, beat

---

225. *LJC*, March 5, 1920 by Dr. Jacob Bernstein-Kohn, p. 20
226. Ibid.
227. *New York Times*, Sept 19, 1919
228. In 1954, the city of Proskurov was renamed Chmielnicky by the Soviets, in commemoration of the 300th anniversary of the treaty negotiated by Ukrainian leader Bogdan Chmielnicky following the Cossack revolt against Poland. Under Chmielnicky's leadership some of the most horrific massacres of Jews until the twentieth century had taken place during that revolt at the hands of the Cossacks.

them with their fists and with iron bars. Trampled them under their feet and stabbed them with bayonets. Some victims were found with thirty-six wounds each. The Cossacks began with the children, tortured them before their parents' eyes and then murdered the parents with weapons soaked in their children's blood. The bodies were found disfigured, mutilated, or beheaded. A countless number of women were violated. The pogroms lasted six days. The cry of the Cossacks was death to the Jews.[229]

In the city of Proskurov, on February 15, 1919, in a matter of hours, 1500 Jews were murdered. Elias Heifetz who authored a detailed report for the Jewish People's Relief Committee of America, assembling hundreds of testimonies about Proskurov:

The mass of the Jews had heard of the Bolshevik revolt which had occurred. Accustomed in recent times to all kinds of firing, they paid no particular attention to the shots which were heard in the morning. It was Saturday and the Orthodox Jews had gone to Synagogue, where they prayed, and then, returning home, sat down to the Sabbath dinner. Many, according to the Sabbath custom, had lain down to sleep. . . . The Cossacks scattered over the Jewish streets in groups of five to fifteen, and with perfectly calm faces entered the houses, took their sabres, and began to cut down all the Jews in the houses without distinction of age or sex. They killed old men, women, and even nursing babies. They not only cut them down with the sword, but also thrust them through with bayonets. They resorted to firing only in case[s where] individuals succeeded in breaking forth into the street. The bullets were sent after them. When news of the beginning of the massacre spread among the Jews, they began to hide in attics and cellars, but the Cossacks dragged them down and killed them. Into the cellars they threw hand grenades.[230]

---

229. *Current Opinion*: January, 1920, p. 88, "America Denounces the Slaughter of Jews in Poland and Ukraine"

230. Elias Heifetz, *The Slaughter of the Jews in the Ukraine in 1919*, Thomas

On May 25, 1926, Petlura was assassinated in a French Café by a watchmaker and former volunteer in the French army, Sholem Schwartzbard, as an act of revenge for the massacres. After a lengthy trial, Schwartzbard was acquitted by a jury on account of the eye-witness testimonies during the trial to the immense suffering of Ukrainian Jewry at the hands of pogromchiks during those post-war years.

While bearing some level of responsibility, it is difficult to completely ascertain the extent of Petlura's guilt since many units were rogue and had acted independently regardless of orders. Evidence that directly implicates him to the horrors is lacking. Furthermore, in an order against anti-Jewish violence, he had stated, "Officers and Cossacks! It is time to know that the Jews have, like the greater part of our Ukrainian population suffered from the horrors of the Bolshevik-Communist invasion and follow the way of truth."[231] How true his intentions were in this statement remains a matter of doubt which may have been more of an effort to assuage Western opinion. A more proactive stance on his part to avert violence might have prevented many pogroms.

Soviet Communism

As Soviet Communists waged war against religion, Judaism was under severe pressure.

Initially, the new government under its leader Vladimir Lenin, denounced anti-Semitism but soon some Jewish Communists, determined to undermine Jewish communal life, were influential in persuading the government to outlaw Jewish organizations. A war would be waged against Jewish practices within the USSR. The Jewish wing of the communists, the *Yevsektzia* was established in order to wage an unrelenting destructive campaign. In the words of the prophet Isaiah,

---

Seltzer, New York, 1921, p. 208

231. Order no. 131, August 26, 1919, Soldiers of the Ukrainian People's Republic Ordered to Respect and Protect the Jews, quoted from *The Jewish Pogroms in Ukraine: Authoritative Statements on the Question of Responsibility for Recent Outbreaks Against the Jews in Ukraine*, Compiled by the Friends of Ukraine Munsey Building, Washington D.C., 1919

foretelling of Jews acting against fellow Jews, "Your destroyers and they that made you waste shall go forth from you."(49:17)

On October 20, 1918, the Commissariat (communist organization) passed a resolution calling for a prohibition of all operating institutions in the Jewish quarter and the *Yevsektzia* organized seizures on synagogues and Jewish Schools.[232] These institutions were often converted into clubs or warehouses.

As the communists defeated their opposition and consolidated power by 1924, they were in control of what became known as the USSR, a vast confederation of Soviet republics.

Over the 1920s, the persecution intensified. The religious life of Soviet Jewry faced a massive crisis.

One of the main promoters of *Yevsektzia* propaganda was Simon Diamanstein 1886–1937, who was an assistant to Josef Stalin, and became editor of the Yiddish journal, *Der Emes* (The Truth). Diamanstein espoused communist propaganda against religion, Judaism and Zionism. He would eventually be executed as other Jewish communists during the purges of Josef Stalin. (1924–1953).

By 1928, ten years after it was formed, the estimated membership of the *Yevsektzia* was at 50,000. The following year, it would be disbanded by Stalin.[233]

But the persecution did not end.

One headline in the Jewish Telegraphic Agency was an example of the decline of the Jewish Community. "Fifty three Russian Synagogues Converted in One Month." The story continues to state that these Synagogues were only in Ukraine, not including White Russia and Central Russia.[234]

In another of many such incidents, the Kiev Great Synagogue was turned into a Workman's Club after a three year fight.[235]

Jews around the world were aware to some extent of the persecution.

---

232. Salo Baron, *The Russian Jew Under Tsars and Soviets*, Schocken Books, New York, 1987, pp. 174–175

233. *JTA*, December 21, 1928

234. *JTA*, November 22, 1929

235. *JTA*, September 8, 1926

Some in the West spoke out in protest.

In one example, Dr. Jochelman, representative of Federation of Ukrainian Jews in Great Britain warned that "The Jews in Soviet Russia face the danger of physical and moral destruction; if no help is extended to them the greatest catastrophe in Jewish history will be unavoidable.[236]

On October 24, 1928, a public rally was held featuring political leaders held at Cooper Union. The mayor, both New York senators and congress members were in attendance. Rabbi Eliyahu Inselbush of the Rabbinical Board which organized the rally stated, "Siberia is now being filled with those who dare to exercise the principle of freedom of worship, as it was in the days of the Czar with those who sought political freedom."[237]

On July 29, 1929, three leading rabbinic luminaries in Eastern Europe, the Chafetz Chaim, the Lubavitcher Rebbe – Rabbi (Yitzchak) Schneerson, and Rabbi Chaim Ozer Grodzinsky, called for a fast day to be held on September 4, the eve of the Hebrew month of Elul, a month designated for introspection before the arrival of the Rosh HaShanah and Yom Kippur holidays. The day of prayer and fasting was for a cessation of persecution of the Jewish religion in the Soviet Union.[238]

The famed Hebrew Author, Chaim Nachman Bialik wrote of Soviet persecution of the Jews, "The most atrocious terrorization is being applied openly and more so secretly against the Hebrew language, the Hebrew culture, Jewish Religion and Zionsim."[239]

In 1930, the pre-eminent sage of that generation, Rabbi Yisrael Meir Kagen HaKohen, otherwise known as the Chafetz Chaim wrote about the immense challenges facing Soviet Jewry. He coauthored with the sage, Rabbi Chaim Ozer Grodzinski, the following letters.

Entitled, "A Call for Help," the first letter appealed for assistance. On the urgent situation facing Russian Jewry, the sages wrote,

---

236. *JTA*, August 25, 1924
237. *JTA*, October 21, 1928
238. *JTA*, July 30, 1929
239. *JTA*, May 26, 1929

My heart faints and hands tremble at the approximately three million Jews in captivity under duress and oppression."[240] "Behold the situation facing the Jews of Russia and the Ukraine is very terrible. May Hashem have mercy. Nearly three million Jews are in deep trouble and distress. . . . Suffering under oppression of the evil *Yevsektzia* whom seek to uproot our holy Torah and to cause the name of Heaven from our mouths by having *Chederim* and Yeshivot closed.[241]

In another letter, an appeal for *Maot Chittim* (charitable funds to procure Passover foods) for Russian Jews without means to procure Matzot for Pesach, the sages warn, "Time is limited and the troubles are great." They ask, "Are we going to sit G-d forbid with our hands folded?"[242]

A letter entitled, "An Announcement to our Jewish Brothers on the Situation in Russia," described the extent of the religious persecution in Soviet Russia.

"Books of the Torah, and books of the Talmud, *tefillin*, and *mezuzot* have been put into flames before everyone to see. The houses of study have been closed, and turned into theatres. Ritual baths have been closed and families have avoided family purity. Many of the Rabbis and teachers of Torah have received long prison sentences and many have been exiled.[243]

The Chafetz Chaim composed a prayer on behalf of Soviet Jewry which states, "We beseech the Merciful and gracious King to redeem the children from destruction and to plead the cause of the helpless for you are the Holy and savior of Israel."[244]

For decades to come, Soviet Jewry would struggle against overwhelming odds to maintain its connection to its Jewish heritage.

Upheaval in Russia, the revolutions of 1917, and the ensuing religious persecution came as a result of World War One.

---

240. Ibid. p. 49
241. *Letters of the Chafetz Chaim*, Vol. 3, p. 49
242. Ibid. p. 53
243. Ibid. p. 50
244. Ibid. p.59

Immigration

The World War sparked the enactment of quotas around the world barring immigration.

In 1917, an immigration restriction bill passed the United States House of Representatives by a vote of 241–126 but it was vetoed by President Wilson. The proposed bill would only have accepted Belgium farmers who came to the US during the war. With war waging throughout Europe, Americans were for the most part in no mood to accept foreigners.

By the end of the war, an atmosphere of isolationism dominated much of America as it had other nations as well.

The severe quotas imposed by the USA with the Immigration Restriction Act of 1921, and the Johnson Reed Act of 1924 upon immigration from Eastern and Southern Europe would remain in effect even as Jewish refugees were desperately seeking shelter from Nazi occupied territories in the late 1930s.

Other nations imposed their own anti-immigration quotas at the time.

The Balfour Declaration and Jewish Statehood

The suffering of Jewry during the war made it all the more apparent to many Jews of the need for a Jewish homeland in the Land of Israel. The Zionist movement had grown significantly among the Jews during the war.

With the issuing of the Balfour Declaration, the hope and expectation was that the realization of Jewish statehood was forthcoming.

The Hebrew writer and prominent Zionist Echad HaAm, otherwise known as Asher Ginsburg, observed following the issuing of the Balfour Declaration, "England's promise for today was far more certain than her promise for the future."[245]

While the British set about improving the infrastructure of Palestine following the war, the military administration governing the land worked against the establishment of a Jewish State.

---

245. *The Maccabaean*, October 1917, p. 434

In one of many hostile measures towards the Zionists, Jerusalem was placed out of bounds to all Jewish soldiers during the holiday of Passover from April 14th to the 22nd of 1919. Colonel Patterson in protest against the measure wrote,

> Jewish soldiers for the first time in their lives in Palestine are barred from the Temple wall of Jerusalem during Passover! Only a Jew can really understand what it meant to these men, and the strain it put on their discipline and loyalty. How provocative and insulting this order was will be better understood when it is realized that the majority of the population of Jerusalem is Jewish, and therefore there could have been no possible reason for excluding Jewish troops belonging to a British unit, while other British troops were freely admitted, more especially as the conduct of the Jewish soldiers was at all times exemplary.[246]

Such gestures against the Zionists would encourage violence at the hands of their opponents.

In March, 1920, the Arab King, Emir Faisal, with the support of the Syrian congress, had declared himself to be in control of all of Syria, in which he included Palestine. During the Passover holiday on April 4, 1920, local Arabs in Jerusalem and nearby towns were primed for confrontation. Inflammatory speeches by extremist leaders called for violence. It was the third day of the Muslim Nebi Musa festival which is accompanied by processions. Thousands had gathered in Jerusalem. Before the festival, notices were displayed around Jerusalem: "The government is with us, Allenby is with us, kill the Jews; there is no punishment for killing the Jews."[247]

In front of Jaffa Gate at the entrance to the Old City of Jerusalem, during a procession, the incitement began.

Aref al-Aref, the editor of *al-Suriya al-Janubiyya*, said, "If we don't use force against the Jews, we will never be rid of them."[248] In re-

---

246. Lt. Col. John Henry Patterson, *With the Judeans in the Palestine Campaign*, Hutchinson and Co., London, 1922, pp. 195–196

247. Ibid.

248. Roberto Mazza, *Jerusalem: From the Ottomans to the British*, I.B. Tauris Pub-

sponse the crowd chanted that they would drink the blood of the Jews.[249] From a balcony, Musa Kazim al-Husseini spoke and the crowd responded, "Palestine is our land, the Jews are our dogs."[250] The riot had begun.

Mobs entered the Old City and set upon the terrified Jewish community. Pillaging, abuse, and murder ensued while the British police stood by. Members of the Jewish Legion were prevented by the British from intervening.

Following almost three days of mayhem, five Jews were murdered, and 211 were wounded, some critically.

The authorities arrested one of the instigators, Amin Al-Husseini, who managed to escape to Damascus. Otherwise, British policy in the immediate aftermath showed little change. They rejected the Jews' demands to dismiss the Arab police who had participated in the pogrom. The British authorities would not even allow over 30 people to accompany remains of victims for burial.

The British also arrested twenty members of the group of Jewish defenders from the Jewish Legion including the leader Zev Jabotinsky for defying British stand-down orders by attempting to intervene before being prevented by the British. Three-year jail sentences were meted out to 19 members. Jabotinsky was tried on the trumped up charges of "banditism, instigating against the people of the Ottoman Empire, and possession of illegal weapons" and received a fifteen year sentence. The sentences were eventually dropped due to an international outcry and opposition from British Members of Parliament.

In absentia, Husseini was given a ten year sentence. However, the next year he returned and was pardoned under an amnesty agreement which was accepted by the new High Commissioner of Palestine on the condition that he would promise to keep the peace.

---

lishers, London, 2009, p. 172, quoted from TNA:PRO WO 32/9614 "Report of the Court of Enquiry into the Riots in Jerusalem During Last April," Jerusalem, 1920

249. Roberto Mazza, *Jerusalem: From the Ottomans to the British*, p. 172, quoted from: Benny Morris, *Righteous Victims*, Vintage, New York, 2001, p. 95

250. Roberto Mazza, *Jerusalem: From the Ottomans to the British*, p. 172, quoted from TNA:PRO WO 32/9614 "Report of the Court of Enquiry into the Riots in Jerusalem During Last April," Jerusalem, 1920

Accusations arose against local British rule of complicity in the pogrom. They attributed their inaction to their own anti-Semitic behavior. In a statement, the *Achdut HaAvodah* (Worker's party) accused British administration officials of, "Allowing agitators to incite the Arab people, allowing them to hold demonstrations. To publish inciting articles in their newspapers, and even to attack Jews while not bringing them to justice."[251] According to another statement by the Worker's party, "The local administration not only failed but placed every impediment in our path. . . . They caused the Arabs to believe that the Jews were left unprotected and as many attacked, they shouted out 'the government is with us.'"[252]

Years later, speaking about the confinement of the Jewish battalion to their camp during the massacre, one member of the Jewish Legion, Leon Chafetz, wrote,

> The Jewish battalion was confined to camp during the massacre in Jerusalem in 1920.[253] The Jewish soldiers were not permitted to defend the lives of their brethren in the Holy City. This edict came from an administration which contained individuals who were outspokenly anti-Semitic, who did not believe in the Balfour Declaration, and who were not free from blame for the tragic events which followed.[254]

It is reasonable to presume by their coordinated lack of response that the British also had prior knowledge of the planned violence. One British administrator, Richard Meinertzhagen maintained that members of the British administration actually incited the violence by encouraging the rioters. According to Meinertzhagen, another British Administrator, [Colonel L.R.E.] Waters-Taylor, met with the Arab leader and soon to be appointed Mufti of Jerusalem, Haj

---

251. *LJC*, August 30, 1920, p. 36

252. Ibid.

253. According to Chiefetz, there were 300 members of the Jewish Legion in Jerusalem at that time. See, "A Page in the History of the Jewish Legion," Leon Chifetz, *The Jewish Ex-Serviceman*, March, 1935, London, p. 21

254. "A Page in the History of the Jewish Legion," Leon Chifetz, *The Jewish Ex-Serviceman*, March, 1935, London, p. 21

Amin Al-Husseini, the Wednesday before the riots and told him he had an opportunity to show the world that the "Arabs of Palestine would not tolerate Jewish domination in Palestine . . . if disturbances of sufficient violence occurred in Jerusalem at Easter."[255] (The following week)

Just weeks later, on April 25, at the San Remo conference in Italy, an agreement was adopted by the post-World War One allied nations affirming the terms of the Balfour Declaration, and the League of Nations article 22 which supported the Balfour Declaration and entrusted Great Britain with a mandate over Palestine with the purpose of establishing a Jewish home in Palestine. This again gave the Zionists cause for hope. However, in a conciliatory gesture to the instigators and at the urging of Arabist members of the British administration, British High Commissioner Herbert Samuel appointed Haj Amin al-Husseini, who Samuel had just pardoned for his role in inciting the pogroms of April 1920, to the position of Mufti (religious leader) of Jerusalem. Husseini's promises to Samuel to promote tranquility were utterly meaningless. Three weeks later, riots were again instigated by the Mufti in Jaffa and Petach Tikvah, which took the lives of 43 Jews. Throughout his life the infamous Mufti of Jerusalem will incite destructive violence in Palestine causing significant damage. He will also forge close relationships with members of the Nazi regime prior to and during World War II, sharing with them common goals as enemies of the Jewish people who actively sought their destruction.

The policies of the local British administrations in Palestine in the aftermath of the war significantly contributed to the rise of Arab terror, and increased challenges faced by the Zionist movement.

In 1920, Jabotinsky told an audience of Zionism supporters in New York,

A wanderer travels at night alone, surrounded by darkness, a biting rain and driving wind hamper his movements: but he is not frightened because from afar he sees light. There is his

---

255. See Colonel Richard Meinertzhagen, *Middle East Diary: 1917–1956*, Thomas Yoseloff, New York, 1960, p. 82

home, warmth and security. We too, Jews and Zionists, may be surrounded by darkness and by ill winds but we know we are going home.[256]

A Demand of the British

On November 11, 1925, crowds filled the Churva synagogue in the Old City of Jerusalem to commemorate the armistice which concluded the First World War, as thunderous cannon fire ushered in a two minute moment of silence. Rabbi Kook then addressed the audience,

> We the Jewish people, have kept silent not only for two minutes but for two thousand years. The nations robbed our Land from us; they plundered our cherished soil; they spilled our blood; and we always kept silent. We suffered for two thousand years of indescribable afflictions, but we kept our peace. . . . Our silence today is our protest, our outcry: Return the theft! Return our holy places, which you took by force![257]

The Unending War

The conclusion of World War One was a respite to future and even greater conflict. The years between the First and Second World Wars were but an interlude as Germany, despite its peoples' immense losses and suffering, would soon prepare itself for another war in the years following the armistice. The German nation maintained its will to fight again.

Following the establishment of the Weimar Democratic Republic in 1919, a communist uprising similar to the Communist Revolution in Russia was attempted. It was a power struggle amid the chaos of post-war Germany. What was known as the Spartacus Revolution, or the January Uprising, was suppressed by Freikorps, paramilitary

---

256. Roman Freulich, *Soldiers of Judea*, p. 151

257. Simchah Raz, *A Prince Among Men*, Translated by Moshe D. Lichtman, Kol Mevaser, Mevaseret Tzion, 2003, pp. 188–189

bands of veterans, who fought on behalf of the moderate Social Democratic Party led by Freidrich Ebert. The leaders of the failed coup, Rosa Luxenburg and Karl Liebknecht, both Jewish, were executed on the same day of their arrest on January 15 by members of the Freikorps.

To the many in the Freikorps, the war never really ended. Not adjusting well to their return to civilian life, members of the Freikorps, sought to live in post-war Germany as part of a military structure. They resented the loss of Germany and bore anger against those they deemed responsible for the defeat. Many of the earlier followers of Nazism soon to come under the leadership of Hitler would be members of the Freikorps.

Was it the Versailles treaty whose terms held Germany accountable for starting the war? The terms may have been harsh but it was far more than a personal affront that motivated German hyper nationalism and the will to fight again.

Provisions in the Versailles treaty ratified after the war infuriated Germans. The Germans were forced to pay massive reparations to the Allies, which would rupture their already severely damaged economy. The War Guilt clause forced them to state that they were responsible for the hostilities; it was a crushing blow to German pride and honor. According to the agreement, the strength of the German army was to be curtailed, and occupation of specific neighboring territories was prohibited. These factors all no doubt added to the resentment of defeat, and to the hyper nationalism that would grip much of Germany in the near future.

But there were also other factors that lead to the rise of Nazism. The charisma and leadership abilities of Adolf Hitler, attracted followers. In addition, there was a vulnerability of Germans during the economic chaos of the Great Depression to seek Nazism, out of desperation, as unemployment rose above fifty percent.

The years which preceded the rise of Nazism were rife with anti-Jewish provocation. Journals and public speakers all joined in the fray accusing Germany's Jews of being the cause of the nation's misfortunes. The popular anti-Jewish canards of the times of Jewish domination and control won wide acceptance and popularity among the German masses, although the Jews numbered only one percent of the population. Slogans such as, "The Jews are our misfortune," and "Germany awake, Jews perish" became popular.

Germany's greatest Jewish industrialist, Walter Rathenau, played an important role organizing the supply of raw materials for Germany during the war. He became the first minister of reconstruction following the war and later the foreign minister of the Weimar Republic. (1919–1933) However, Rathenau soon became the target of tirades, many of which were anti-Semitic, and death threats. Eventually assassinated by German nationalists on June 24, 1922, he noted in 1916 that, "The more Jews die in this conflict, the more persistent will their opponents complaints that the Jews did nothing but sit behind the front profiteering from the war. The hatred will double and triple."[258]

Rabbi Leopold Rosenak observed that after the war, returning German Jewish soldiers "encountered unexpected anti-Semitism. They were affected so much deeper."[259]

As accusations against the Jews intensified after the war, Rabbi Rosenak confronted the anti-Semitic attacks. He published a pamphlet, "Truth and Justice" which refuted the invective, testifying to the contributions of German Jewry to all aspects of German life. He also confronted anti-Semitic leaders at public gatherings at great personal risk.[260]

On October 27, 1919, the Union of Jewish Clubs noting the rise in post-war anti-Semitism, declared, "Let the anti-Semites try by any and all means to cut us to the quick, they will not be able to tear our love of Fatherland from our hearts."[261]

By 1923, the first official Nazi pogrom had taken place in Nuremburg. Placards were distributed that read, "Strike them [the Jews] down like dogs."[262]

The director of the Central-Verein, (German Jewish organization) Ludwig Hollander, protested the exclusion of a rabbi from a cere-

258. Zeit online #42, 1996, p. 2, Amos Elon, *The Pity of it All*, p. 338

259. Minnie Rosenak, *The Rosenaks of Bremen*, p. 13

260. Ibid. *The Rosenaks of Bremmen*, p. 22

261. Ruth Pierson, *German Jewish Identity in the Weimar Republic, Ph.D dissertation*, Yale University, 1970, p. 251

262. *JTA*, November 3, 1924, "First pogrom on German soil in Nuremberg."

mony commemorating Germany's war dead, stating that the exclusion changed nothing in the "moral conception" of their fatherland.[263] At a R.J.F. (Reich Federation of Jewish Front Soldiers) convention in Rhineland 1925, a speaker, Jewish Parliament member Ludwig Haas stated, "It was as German soldiers that we defend ourselves against those who drag our honor through the gutter – and our Germenality is our honor."[264]

Not long after, before the political rise of Nazism in 1933, Haas advised his son to leave Germany and go "as far away as you can."[265] In 1929, Ludwig Hollander declared, "German Jews – Jewish Germans constitute parts of the German people and for all future time members of the German people."[266]

By 1932, the ex-Kaiser told his son to support Adolf Hitler. At a Nazi meeting in Erfurt, Prince Wilhelm related that his father "officially authorized him to propagate Nazi ideas, and to stand as a Nazi candidate for the Prussian Parliament."[267] This was the same Kaiser who pronounced that all Germans were brothers at the beginning of the war.

The ex-Kaiser also stated regarding the Jews, "Let no German ever forget this or rest until these parasites have been extirpated and exterminated from German soil."[268] Less than a year later, on January 30, 1933, Hitler became chancellor of Germany.

General Ludendorff who had promised the Jews of Poland protection and freedom and had so many dealings with many members of the Jewish community during the German occupation of Poland became an early supporter of Adolf Hitler. His support added legitimacy to the small but growing Nazi movement in its earlier days. Ludendorff was a participant in the failed Nazi coup of 1923, the Beer Hall Putsch. Later that year, he published an article in leading nationalist newspapers in which he lists enemies to be fought

---

263. Ibid. p. 252
264. Ibid. p. 273
265. JM Berlin. De.
266. Ibid. p. 275
267. *JTA*, April, 11, 1932
268. Peter Pulzer, *Jews and the German State*, Wayne State University Press, 2003, Detroit, MI, p. 214

when nationalists will come to power. He lists the inner enemies as communism, pacifism, Marxism, particularism, separatism, parliamentarianism and the Jews. In the article, Ludendorff paid special attention to the Jews whom he refers to as "parasites on the German body politic."[269]

On the Western Front, a Jewish captain in a German infantry battalion, Hugo Guttmann, nominated a corporal under his command – Adolf Hitler, the company runner, for the Iron Cross, and successfully lobbied on his behalf. This was an unusual decoration for a corporal. After Hitler came to power in 1933, Guttmann publicly stated that he pinned the medal on him. The Nazis objected denying a Jew could have done it and Guttmann was arrested. He was taken into custody three times before he was allowed to leave for the United States in 1934.[270]

After the war, plaques dedicated to heroes who fell on battlefields marked synagogues of each town. Memorial services were held annually by Jewish organizations. Even after the Nazi rise to power in January, 1933, there were still attempts by some Jews to hold memorials. By a decree issued on October 21, 1935, the names of Jews were no longer permitted to be placed on memorials. Jewish memorials upon Jewish institutions were being removed. By Kristallnacht, the night of broken glass, November 9–10, 1938, as synagogues under the Reich were destroyed, and thousands of Jewish men were rounded up and sent to concentration camps, most of the existing memorial plaques were destroyed.

The German military campaign waged in the East from the beginning of the war in 1914 was a prelude to the Nazi slaughter of Jewry thirty years later. Some of the same troops who interacted with Jewish communities during the German occupation of Poland and Lithuania during the First World War would become leaders in the SS during World War Two directing the massacres of those Jews whom they had previously encountered. Kurt Daluege was the SS chief of the uniformed police, Paul Blobel who served on the Eastern front in WWI became commanding officer Superkommando-4a of

---

269. *JTA*, November 5, 1923
270. Gilbert, *Jews in the Twentieth Century*, p. 74

the Einstazgruppen (Nazi Murder squads). Blobel was in command at the Babi Yar massacre of September 29–30, 1941, where 33,771 Jews were murdered.

The historian Yaffa Eliach related the reaction of citizens on her hometown, Eishyshock, Poland, to the arrival of German troops during the Second World War.

> On the basis of their experiences in German captivity, most of the World War One veterans had great faith in the German respect for law and order, and did their fellow residents of the town of Eishyshock, who had spent the better part of two years under a very peaceful German occupation. Thus, the "new Germans" of World War II would prove worthy heirs to the "good Germans" [gutte deitschen] of World War I.[271]

When those "new Germans" and their Lithuanian collaborators murdered 4,000 people in Eishyshock, their victims included most of the World War One veterans who had so highly praised the civility of their fathers."[272]

The Versailles Treaty

The Versailles treaty was a failure. Its terms which were intended to control the might of Germany were not imposed. Germany rebuilt its army and invaded lands forbidden to them all in violation of the Treaty with impunity.

The Versailles Treaty of June 28, 1919, was meant to punish Germany for its role in the First World War. It was also supposed to curb German military might to prevent future conflict. As any agreement, it was only as good as the parties' willingness to enforce its terms.

With World War One and its horrors in recent memory, nations did not want to prepare for war. Many sought refuge in the wishful thinking that Hitler could or would be reasonable. Britain was

---

271. Yaffa Eliach, *There Once Was a World: A 900-Year Chronicle of the Shtetle of Eishyshok*, Back Bay Books, New York, 1999, p. 223

272. Eliach, p. 223

suffering the effects of the Great Depression and was not in a war preparation mode. America was also in the midst of the great depression. It had joined the war late in 1917, but was instrumental in defeating the Central Powers. It subsequently and then reverted back to its earlier pre-war isolationist policies. But much of German society and their chancellor Adolf Hitler were on a different course.

By 1935, the Versailles Treaty was of no value in containing the military aspirations of Nazi Germany, as its provisions calling for the demilitarization of Germany were flagrantly violated. The treaty stated that Germany should have a limited army with no submarines, military aviation, German General Staff, or army conscription. The Germans had it all. An air force of two thousand five hundred planes, an army of three hundred thousand troops with an announcement by Hitler that he was imposing a draft in order to increase the army size to five-hundred and fifty-thousand.[273]

In 1936, German troops marched into the Rhineland of Germany to militarily reoccupy a zone specifically prohibited by Versailles. Germany also reclaimed sovereignty and fortified the tiny neutral but strategic island of Helgoland, another violation. Yet through it all there was no international opposition to Hitler.

As the Versailles agreement was disregarded, Hitler intensified the brutal German dictatorship threatening non-Aryans. Among a host of repressive measures, the Nuremburg Laws of 1935 censored Jews from German society.

The world's lack of attention to the threat of Hitler also emboldened the aggressiveness of other dictators. In 1935 Italy's fascist leader Benito Mussolini invaded Ethiopia murdering tens of thousands of civilians and used mustard gas against them. In an impassioned appeal before the League of Nations which declared Italy the aggressor but took no action, Haile Salassie, the Emperor of Ethiopia stated, "Are states going to set up a terrible precedent of bowing before force?"[274] But his words went unheeded and the march to war intensified.

The horrific events of the First World War were a prelude to the

---

273. *Literary Digest*, July 26, 1935, p. 11 "Scrap of Paper"
274. Speech before League of Nations, June 30, 1936

Second World War and so many horrors of the twentieth century to follow.

One century later, the world still lives in the shadow of the dark days of "The Great War" of 1914–1918. The threat of war still looms large with new highly technological forms of weaponry but with old hatreds. Mankind still faces dire challenges posed by those who seek to exercise their lust for power, many of whom today are motivated by religious fanaticism and nationalism.

The First World War led to the transformation of Jewish life. As a result of the Russian retreats with the accompanying mass expulsions of Jews, Jewish communities were ripped from their homes and traumatized. The changes in Russia following the Russian Revolution led to Soviet totalitarianism as religious observance among European Jewry continued to decline due to persecution. The post-war outbreak of anti-Semitism in European nations shattered the continued hopes of many Jews for acceptance and equality despite their devoted service and sacrifices to their respective nations. Instead, they most often experienced exclusion and rejection.

The emergence of national entities with the fall of empires and the struggles for independence resulted in massacres, which were often even more severe than those during the war. Post-war Germany was accompanied by the rise of extreme German nationalism and the birth and growth of Nazism.

Amid the bleak and ominous picture, hopes for Jewish statehood were raised following the issuing of the Balfour Declaration and the allied conquest of Palestine. The search for belonging led some to Zion. To many, due to the immense dangers Jewry was facing, the need for the restoration of the Jews to their ancestral homeland seemed increasingly dire.

In today's world, global conflicts can still be traced to their origins in the First World War. Jewry, as well, is still immensely impacted by those horrific and traumatic times, which led to subsequent persecution over the 20th century, and also to the rebirth of the State of Israel.

About the Author

LARRY DOMNITCH has taught history at Touro College and is the author of *The Cantonists: The Jewish Children's Army of the Tsar* and *The Jewish Holidays: A Journey through History*, as well as many articles, including in the *Algemeiner*, *The Jewish Press*, and *Israel National News*.